YES, we can...
...rewrite the Australian Constitution

Klaas Woldring

Cover Design by BookPOD

Printed and bound in Australia by BookPOD

A Catalogue-in-Publication is available from the National Library of Australia.

ISBN: 978-1-925457-75-9

Thank you!

Here is a big thank you to my family as well as to members of the Beyond Federation group for encouraging me to write this short book. It was originally conceived, quite long ago, as Government by Judges, based on my view (in the 1980s) that most really important decisions in the political sphere in Australia are decided by courts, judges and all kinds of judiciary or quasi-judiciary bodies. In mid-2017 a daughter asked me "Dad what actually happened to your idea to write a book about that years ago and for which you collected a lot of research material?" Good question! Then the Section 44 drama started, a trigger, and I went back to the collected clippings, papers and other books that I did write in recent years. A lot of new relevant material came to light as well much of it provided by other family members during the Christmas holidays. Thanks also to Jim Snow, former MP for the Bellwether seat of Eden-Monaro, for reading a first draft. If Australia was to adopt proportional representation - party list there would be no more Bellwether seats but it could lead to a Bellwether movement for a new Constitution for Australia.

Preface

Many Australians do not know much about the Australian Constitution. Given the relatively peaceful society, steady economic growth since WWII, large migrant population and lack of easy to understand information, this is not so surprising. Thus, a generalised view has taken root, amongst some at least, that "the Constitution has served Australia well" or "it cannot be so bad that it needs to be overhauled completely". There is also a view that "Australians are conservative and therefore would not be keen to change the Constitution or governance systems. The current Prime Minister keeps saying that. Frankly, that may apply to a very small minority only. What is true is that ignorance about the Constitution and political processes and governance systems is widespread. But then there are also those Australians who are quite familiar with the Constitution, know that there is much wrong with the document, but believe, are convinced even, that major change is extremely difficult. It simply cannot be done, they claim! We have to live with it! And then, on top of that, there are certainly several scholars and journalists who have tried very hard to present alternatives, regrettably, thus far, all in vain. What the average Australian does know and is concerned about is the gravely diminished trust in our politicians. But the connection between the Constitution and, more generally, governance systems and the lack of confidence in the politicians is hardly understood. In part, this book aims to be a response to all of these views.

There are undoubtedly serious problems with the Australian Constitution. It certainly is not just the language of the late 19th century. It is the structure of the national state, the many vital issues not covered, due to the social, economic, political and environmental changes and values since 1901. In particular, the totality of associated governance systems, like for instance the electoral systems, has made meaningful reforms basically impossible. Moreover, the political system itself is in real turmoil. Prime Ministers come and go. Reasonably optimistic expectations of the current Prime Minister, Malcolm Turnbull, stranded as a result of the factional party system. How could this Republican be muzzled by the conservative faction of his own Party? Why was he unable to effectively appeal to the middle ground of Australian politics? And why is the Leader of the Opposition, Bill Shorten, while the ALP is constantly leading in the polls, only marginally acceptable as alternative Prime Minister?

The Australian Constitution is essentially an archaic colonial document, a law of the British Parliament in 1901. This is no longer a Constitution for a multicultural society, if it ever was. In terms of promoting democracy it is of no assistance. It created a Federation that is no longer fit for purpose. The constitutional and political cultures are drenched in Anglo-Celtic and Westminster political practices and systems of yesteryear. In spite of the Australia Act, adopted by the British Government and the Commonwealth in 1986, confirming Australia as an independent state, the 1901 basic set of rules has hardly changed. Phil Cleary, a former MP for the seat of Wills, the Independent who also lost his seat as a result of a Section 44 ruling 25 years ago, recently wrote that "in an immigrant country our Constitution is farcical" (*SMH* 31.10.2017). Sadly, it is indeed and it has to change, the sooner the better. This cumulative effect over 117 years is recognised by many constitutional academics and lawyers but only the very brave few have dared to suggest that a complete rewrite is now required. Among those few there may still be some who maintain that the federal structure should be kept in place. The position taken in this text is that the Federation has also become a costly, dysfunctional relic of the past and that decentralisation, its often-assumed remaining advantage, can be achieved much more effectively in other ways. It is hopeful that a series of reformist essays by mostly younger law academics has been published by ANU recently (September 2017). It may assist in opening up debate. Their encouragement to involve the public more directly in reforms debate about the Constitution should be noted particularly.

Scott Lambert, a former section manager in the schools area of the Australian Government's education portfolio, writing three pieces for the eMagazine The Mandarin in recent months, has supported the value of "a bold inspiring proposal for the adoption for a new Constitution". He argued that this could succeed where proposals for modest amendments have floundered. Quite so! URL references are placed in the Bibliography under the heading "Articles".

The teaching about the Constitution in detail has been confined to the few, mostly students at Law Schools of the universities. Exposure such as has happened at High Schools has been perfunctory, limited to explanations of how it works, not including a critical examination of how it doesn't work, why it "cannot" be updated, or how it could be improved. The description "our democracy" is frequently associated with the Constitution. Sadly, such democracy as does exist is hardly protected in the Constitution. Meanwhile, there is little doubt that Australia is rapidly becoming a plutocracy, although always presented as a democracy, a particularly undesirable development. An effort to suggest a rewrite of the Constitution may seem almost absurd to many. But it well may be the only way to achieve real change! The author is not a constitutional lawyer but a retired Associate Professor in politics and management, born in the Netherlands, who became an Australian citizen in 1969. The approach in this short book specifically is to reach and inform the general public about basics. Without a much wider, common sense understanding of the issues the necessary groundswell for constitutional and related political system, changes may not be generated. The major parties have no policy agenda for major constitutional change – apart from the ALP's very minimalist Republic a prospect which is currently further removed from the people's mind than in 1999. Frankly, even the ALP is deeply steeped in the conservative governance systems. Both the major parties, as they currently operate, are in fact very much part of the problem of stagnation. This is therefore a short, non-academic book aimed to convince readers that a sovereign people should be able to rewrite the basic rules that govern their society to match its values and aspirations. This is especially so when amending their existing archaic and frozen Constitution, is demonstrably no longer a viable option.

Can Australia do that? Of course: YES, we can! A sovereign people can rewrite their entire Constitution, in one go. Only the people and their genuine representatives can do that. That is the essence of sovereignty! That is the ultimate statement of legal and political independence. But first we have to grasp the basics of why we are in this predicament and outline possible strategies generating a widespread desire for the changes to be made.

Contents

Introduction

If Australia is to progress further this is not just a matter of creating jobs, accommodating still more people in the major cities, handling the economy well and turn around the growing inequality. There is certainly a lot at stake for Australia in a complex world where rapidly growing inequality and huge refugee movements are demanding much attention, where climate change and energy prices are constantly in the news, demanding the attention of consumers, media and governments. There is the subservience to the US which, after having become involved in several unnecessary and avoidable wars as an ally of that country, is increasingly questioned. The Australian Constitution and its Westminster Conventions allow commitments to participate in wars without serious advice from either the people or the Parliament. This is a most undemocratic situation surely. The Prime Minister, *not even mentioned in the Constitution,* can decide for the nation to commit Australia to a war, basically decided on, and even caused by a US President. This has happened several times. Now the Australian Government has to deal with President Donald Trump and a mounting threat from North Korea. Only recently this new US President was elected by the Electoral College, based on a winner-take-all federal system designed for that particular purpose. His opponent, the Democrat Hillary Clinton, actually gained 2.8 million more votes than Trump, a clear majority. Cause of problem: a poor democratic system!

Australia is seriously struggling in many of these areas. It is a small nation in numbers in a very large country surrounded by a great variety of different societies, cultures and interests. The written federal Constitution is now supposedly a Constitution of an independent nation but the rules of this Constitution are lagging behind most of all. This has come to light again like a bolt from a seemingly blue sky, unexpectedly, with the Section 44 drama. These ground rules determine who can be a Member of the House Representatives or the Senate and who not. The rule laid down in 1901, in Section 44, was that one could "not have allegiance to a foreign power", which meant, at the time, one had to be a British subject alone, a citizen of the British Empire. The concept of an "Australian citizenship" did not even formally exist until 1948. During 2017 it transpired that several MPs actually had "dual nationality", most of them being completely unaware of this. The High Court ruled on this issue applying the so-called Black Letter approach, arguing that the law had to be applied literally, as it stood, even though this was clearly an example of a provision that applied to very different circumstances. Soon several Senators and federal MPs found themselves without a job and had to be replaced by Senate candidates who had missed out in the 2016 Double Dissolution election or, in the lower house, via by-elections, e.g. in the NSW seats named New England and Bennelong. The very slender parliamentary majority by the governing Coalition in the House of Representatives was threatened. A change of Government suddenly became a possibility for the struggling Government headed by Malcolm Turnbull. This unexpected, for the Government unwelcome disruption, keeping Australians in suspense for several months, was primarily the result of the Constitution not keeping up with a changing society while being guarded over, at least on this occasion, by an inflexible and impractical High Court, sitting as the country's Constitutional Court.

We need to go back to the political upheaval that came to a head over the Constitution in 1975. The growth period of the post-war period and large-scale immigration, from many countries, had provided strong employment and economic growth during 23 years of Liberal and National Party Coalition Government. However, it started to come apart during the Gorton and McMahon governments, with Prime Ministers changing in rapid succession. The ALP came to power in 1972 with the reformist Gough Whitlam as Prime Minister, campaigning under the motto: "It's time". Few people would have disagreed with that. It was in fact time for many and for major changes. However, it proved to be a very brief term of strong, progressive government after a period of stagnation and directionless government. Some major policy changes that were quickly introduced by Whitlam and his team, within a three-year period, crashed on the conservative mindset and, especially, on the poorly adapted, basically unadapted Constitution. The major changes required were much further away than anyone could guess then. The process of governance system change had hardly begun. However, increasingly Australia was becoming a multicultural society and an independent country. Issues like social inclusion, later, political inclusion in a constitutional and political system that was a problematic mixture of the British Westminster system and the US federal structure, presented challenges. Updating these systems increasingly proved virtually impossible.

In spite of various extensive political and academic contributions virtually nothing had changed in the Australian Constitution since 1901. Sadly, this continued after the drama of 1975 when the Whitlam government was removed by the conservative forces, spearheaded by the uncertain Governor General, Sir John Kerr. Kerr apparently used his "Reserve Powers", so he believed, and probably acted also on behalf of British advice Australia has learned recently. This drama only resulted in a very wordy amendment to Section 15, named

Constitution Alteration (Senate Casual Vacancies) 1977, introduced by the succeeding Fraser Government. Governor-General Kerr's decision had happened after two conservative State Premiers (NSW and Queensland) had broken the constitutional Convention to replace retiring Senators by members of their own party. Essentially, this was piecemeal tinkering. It was approved as such in a referendum in May,1977. In the aftermath of that constitutional crisis a period of introspection did occur in Australia in political and academic circles. Chapter 3 of this text will deal with that period. The dissatisfaction post-1975 was subdued though, mainly as a result of Fraser's meliorism. Notably, his Government did not reverse any of the main Whitlam reforms. For readers less familiar with Australian politics a list of federal Governments and their Prime Ministers will now be stated for the period 1972 – 2017:

Gough Whitlam (ALP)	1972–1975
Malcolm Fraser (Coalition)	1975–1983
Bob Hawke (ALP)	1983–1991
Paul Keating (ALP)	1991–1996
John Howard (Coalition)	1996–2007
Kevin Rudd (ALP)	2007–2010
Julia Gillard (ALP)	2010 – 2013
Kevin Rudd (ALP)	2013
Tony Abbott (Coalition)	2013–2015
Malcolm Turnbull (Coalition)	2015–present

Economic progress and continued mass immigration characterised the Hawke and Keating years. It also meant an often uncomfortable, part-acceptance of neo-liberal aims such as the privatisation of the Commonwealth Bank – and several other privatisations. However, a more comprehensive multicultural society emerged even though multiculturalism hardly penetrated the political system. The Australian electoral and political systems were also particularly slow in electing women to Parliament in anywhere near representative numbers. The electoral system was also partly to blame for that reality. The ALP did somewhat better here than the Coalition and elected the first woman Prime Minister in 2010, Julia Gillard.

However, a comprehensive 900-page study of the Constitution was undertaken by a high-level committee, deliberating from 1985 - 1988, comprising Gough Whitlam (former PM), Sir Rupert Hamer (former Liberal Party Premier of Victoria), Professors Enid Campbell and Leslie Zines, and Sir Maurice

Byers. Their comprehensive Report resulted in four sensible Referendum questions which, sadly, were all rejected in 1988. The recommendations of this Commission were far-reaching and concentrated heavily on human rights. The result showed up the enormous gap between reformers, on the one hand, and political parties on the other hand. Especially the Coalition parties proved exceptionally conservative and dogmatic. Initially they supported three of the four proposals but they ended up campaigning against all of them. This adversarial situation made it very clear that constitutional amendment referendums have no chance of being approved unless the major parties agree. Thus, at the outset we can establish that there are at least three main factors which have prevented the updating of the colonial Constitution:

1. Clause 128, requiring a national majority as well as a majority in a majority of states (four out of six), a condition the smaller states demanded in the 1890s.

2. The adversarial two-party system itself – a result of the electoral system.

3. The constitutional requirement that only federal politicians can propose federal constitutional amendments.

Nevertheless, an outstanding, courageous and somewhat unexpected judgement came from the High Court in 1992 when it decided, by a majority of 6 : 1 in the Eddie Mabo case, that the concept of Terra Nullius was wrong and that Indigenous people could claim land rights if continued prior occupancy could be established. Clearly, Australia was not an empty country when the British claimed New South Wales in 1770, as was apparently assumed or the Indigenous people were not considered as citizens or even as humans in any European sense. However, the Indigenous people had lived here for a very long time, possibly for 65,000 years. At least that erroneous doctrine was removed, but this judgement did not amend the Constitution in relation to Sections that discriminate against the Indigenous people (Sections 25 and 51xxvi) which have been the subject of much recent controversy, discussion and interesting new constitutional proposals, the Uluru Statement, regrettably soon rejected by the Turnbull Government.

To date only 8 of 44 amendment proposals have been successful. The number of possible and desirable proposals is greater, probably much greater than 44, but the fear of failure is such that only very likely successful proposals, supported by both major parties, are put to the voters. No Government likes to risk failure of a costly Referendum unless a promise made in an election campaign of course, as John Howard did in the 1996 election and was then elected. Regrettably, the actual proposal he put forward had little chance of being approved and failed. Therefore, further piecemeal tinkering clearly makes no sense. Given the current dismal state of Australia's political system at least two measures need to be considered.

1. A complete rewrite of the Australian Constitution need to be undertaken as soon as possible following a totally Independent Inquiry. Serving politicians should not be members of the Commission of Inquiry. Obviously, if still really useful, uncontroversial sections of the existing Constitution can be left in the new draft but much of it should go or replaced. The notion that Australia needs to remain in the Westminster mould for some reason, while some practices are clearly counterproductive, is unhelpful to say the least. Including some independent foreign experts on the committee should be helpful.

2. It would help if the Governor-General adopted an active and innovative role to start this process. The existing **written** Constitution actually provides for this possibility. In spite of the fact that in the Westminster system the Governor-General has a largely symbolic role, as a principal advisor to the Queen (of Australia), this person has sufficient executive capacity to intervene – on the basis of the "Reserve Powers" in any case, whatever the constitutional conventions. This is especially so as it is very obvious now that neither major party is able to achieve constitutional reform! They have had three decades to act. Some would say really since 1975. Where to from here?

This leads us to further important introductory issues. First, in the early to mid-noughties, some 15 years ago now, a number of excellent texts were published that seriously discussed the need for a new Constitution in Australia. I contributed to some of them. But nothing happened, the major political parties did not take even preliminary steps in that direction. Why would a call for major change now be any more successful? Obviously, the initiatives and political clout need to come from elsewhere. First of all, it needs to come through discussion by the general public and in the media, particularly the ABC and SBS as public broadcasters, perhaps especially from multicultural Australia. Secondly, it has to be taken up by mass organisations like GetUp and/or similar activist groups. Thirdly the political clout can come, at least in part, from minor parties and Independents represented in the Senate, a result of proportional representation. The Xenophon group, Greens and several Independents already have the balance of power there and have developed political clout and negotiating power in several policy areas. As Australia is preparing for a general election in 2019, or even earlier, constitutional reform can be placed on their agenda items. Fourthly, these ideas can be financially supported by corporations and financiers with an interest in such reforms like, e.g. Dick Smith. Fifthly, a new political party with Constitutional Reform as its principal objective could be started aiming to gain representation in the Senate. Section 53 of the existing Constitution, however deficient, ends as follows: *Except as provided in this Section, the Senate shall have equal power with the House of Representatives in respect of all proposed laws.* The exceptions refer to laws appropriating revenue or moneys, or imposing taxes. A new Constitution could easily reduce costs especially if it means that the costly Federation is replaced. In any case the power of the Senate could be increased greatly by the further growth of minor parties and Independents favouring a new Constitution to develop a new Constitution for Australia.

Is it conceivable at all that the current political class could contribute to greater popular participation in decision-making following the success of the Same Sex Marriage postal vote? Recently the Australian Republic Movement, although still committed to a minimalist position, has suggested that crucial questions could be dealt with in a similar fashion provided that the Government accepts the outcome. Though interesting as an example, when it comes to constitutional changes in the end the change has to happen via the mechanism provided in Section 128 - and that has been the principal stumbling block all along. Nevertheless, the government could present a series of governance system changes to the voting public, as options. It would almost certainly find that Australians are far less conservative than claimed. It would then also find that the voters, when properly informed, would favour massive changes impossible to achieve with the current constitutional system!

The distrust of the politicians, as the political class, together with the failure to achieve governance system change as described above, has also resulted in proposals for the renewal of the democracy which may be far-reaching but are relatively untested. Compared to what is suggested in this text they are very idealistic, directly related as they are to the poor performance of many politicians and the political class as a whole in a number of Western democracies. It is essential that these advocacies are mentioned and briefly discussed here, up front, to assess their credibility or part-credibility and their achievability. E.g., four theorists were discussed in an article by Luke Slattery in the *Good Week-end* (23.6.2016) under the title *"Silvertail subversives: the men aiming to change a system in which they prosper".* Another recent text which deals with that very issue even more directly and comprehensively is Brett Hennig's *The End of Politicians - Time for a Real Democracy*, Unbound, 2017.

Of the four interviewed by journalist Slattery three are men of independent means who have promoted and financed voluntary organisations pursuing alternative democratic ideals. The fourth one, Richard Walsh is a well-known former 1970s activist, of modest means, who has published a book *Reboot – Democracy make-over to empower Australian voters*, MUP, 2017.

Walsh writes: *"If you want real change, change the system."* Bravo! He proposes several solutions, some obviously sensible (and long overdue), others more speculative and/or utopian, some are missing perhaps but his is a short book. First up is Australia's electoral system, which, in seven of our nine lower houses, is based on individual Single Member Districts (SMDs). Walsh is attracted to the Hare-Clark proportional representation system, more especially to the original ideas of the Englishman Thomas Hare, in the mid-19th century. This system was partly applied in Tasmania; first in 1896 and later, in 1907, extending it to five districts of six members; later also in the ACT. The multi-member district base of the system has undoubtedly great advantages. It results in a much more cooperative (non-adversarial) culture but Walsh omits to mention that later adaptations of Hare-Clark in Australia have resulted in many serious problems, especially in the Senate, largely the result of compulsory preferencing. He does refer encouragingly to the introduction of a form of PR party list system in New Zealand (MMP, two votes), which he recommends for Australia. Strangely, there is no mention of the much more widely used PR – Party List system in many non-English-speaking countries – no less than 86 of them – whereby voters have a wide choice but only one vote.

A further recommendation is the abolition of the Senate which would of course would require a far-reaching amendment to the Australia's federal Constitution, really a re-write. As a Republican Walsh says Australia's needs a new President and this official should be popularly elected (from six candidates) as well as a 12-person elected Council to assist him/her, elected from 20 candidates by preferential vote. The President would have largely symbolic role. As to the new House of Representatives Walsh recommends two categories of MPs: those elected by "open" or "closed" electors.

The other three discussed are Transfield Holdings managing director and New Democracy Foundation head Luca Belgiorno-Nettis; Melbourne property developer and publisher Morry Schwartz; and Sydney venture capitalist Mark Carnegie.

Slattery describes: "They are the silvertail subversives determined to shake up a moribund political culture. Their prestige in the corporate and cultural worlds insulates them from charges of left-wing ratbaggery but leaves them vulnerable to blue-collar scorn and the scepticism of a tall-poppy-scything society innately hostile towards intellectual elites. Or elites, full stop. **Something unforeseen has happened** to Western democracy in the early decades of the 21st century, and professors and pundits around the globe are struggling to make sense of it. Seven years after the empty democratic promises of the Arab Spring, a bleak Occidental Autumn has settled over the landscape. Populism is on the rise. And the political class – statesmanship itself – is on the nose". The future of mainstream politics may depend on its capacity for renewal and reform, a point both Walsh and Luca Belgiorno-Nettis are keen to drive home.

Belgiorno-Nettis referred to a national survey done by New Democracy, in March 2017, in which 81% felt that "everyday people should play a bigger part in government decisions that affect their lives". The big reform suggested is citizen juries of randomly selected people who will be asked to debate, deliberate and recommend policy to arms of government. He referred to Athenian Assembly in Greece as an earlier example in fifth century BC and provides the technical name *Sortition* for this system. Athens was a small city state where about one third had the vote, excluding women, the slaves and the many foreigners. Apparently, there are no comparable examples in the world of the 19th and 20th century. However, there are some limited examples of randomly selected citizen assemblies in a number of countries dealing with specific, delegated decision-making processes on particular issues, including financial and tax issues.

Morry Schwartz, a well-known publisher of note, starting with "Outback Press" in the Whitlam area, later, for example, *The Quarterly Essay* and *The Monthly*. He is a democrat and a Republican and said, "we don't need wholesale changes but we do need an Australian President".

It is fear that motivates Mark Carnegie to speak out publicly on troubles to which most people of his kind, enjoying the view from the first-class lounge and the marina, are inured. "Fear for my kids", he explained.

He speaks regularly at conferences and in the media. His ideal Australia is a more equal Australia. It's not, though, a levelling instinct that drives him; more a case of broadening the opportunities to rise. The alternative to greater equality of opportunity, he insists, is "leaving a whole lot of social potential on the scrap-heap". Like Walsh and Belgiorno-Nettis, Carnegie is frustrated by the political culture, particularly the choke-hold of political parties on ideas – he calls it "vote politics". But he has no whiz-bang structural reform to promote. In fact, he's not so much concerned with the structure of government as society: social capital – the economist's term for the social fabric – is one of his big themes.

Finally, this bring us to the informative new text by Brett Hennig (2017) *The End of Politicians - Time for a Real Democracy*, Unbound. Much of this book is devoted to the philosophy of developing a true democracy rather than improving a "representative democracy". That concept is actually considered as "a contradiction in terms" because the representatives are failing in their duty to actually represent the people who voted them in. But in other parts the randomly selected citizen assemblies are also presented as a new, or further, "mutation" of democracy. In later chapters examples of stratified randomly selected, citizen assemblies for limited or local government purposes are provided. According to Professor Erik Olin Wright, author of *Envisioning Real Utopias*, the Hennig book "provides a powerful critique of the democratic deficits in all forms of electoral democracy". Reading the book over Christmas 2017 this is not quite correct. In actual fact, the book of 18 chapters, deals primarily with the electoral systems of the UK, the US and Australia and finds them rightly deficient in many respects, especially in terms of democratic representation. Their elections are largely based on the single-member-district (SMD) system that originated in Britain and was exported to the US and Australia, and to some other English-speaking countries as well (e.g., South Africa, where it greatly contributed to the emergence of Apartheid from 1948). There are many references to well-known authors on the subject most of whom also originate from these three countries. There are graphs and statistics covering most democracies, or pseudo-democracies, in the world, and of trends such as the, to the author, unexpected survival and strong growth of democracies after WWII. There are also some references to other electoral systems in other countries which throw up important unanswered questions:

> " *In plurality-majority voting systems, such as that of the UK, one candidate is elected from each area, resulting in a parliament typically dominated by two leading parties. In such systems equality refers to an equality of initial opportunity to vote. In proportional voting systems, as used, for example in the Netherlands, multiple politicians are usually elected from extended areas in proportion to the votes gained (which often results in many parliamentary parties, and hence coalition governments). The quality in proportional systems refers to the equality of influence on the outcome. In both systems, each vote has an equal value in theory, although in plurality-majority systems it is obvious that many more votes have no value in practice, as they will not contribute to the composition of parliament. The analysis of the political inequality of certain*

15

votes could go even further: election results in a UK-type system often hinge on the outcome of a handful of marginal seats, so the choices of swinging voters may be crucial, making their votes very powerful indeed." Hennig, p. 17

Some of the great contributions of the Dutch-American Professor Arend Lijphardt are mentioned in Hennig's book although Lijphardt's very relevant work is not listed in the Select Biography **(see Footnote at the end of Bibliography of this text).** As the proposed remedy by the Sortition Foundation to the current political malaise in the three countries may gain some support, in spite of acknowledged huge practical problems, this description in the Hennig book clearly provides a different alternative:

"Proportional representation systems are an alternative that leads to many more parties attracting votes and obtaining parliamentary seats. Figure 4 compares the percentage of seats that the three major parties or coalitions received in recent national elections to the legislative house of parliaments in the UK, Australia, Germany and the Netherlands. The discrepancy between each pair of columns highlights how unrepresentative a system is, when a party received disproportionally more (or fewer) seats than votes. Wherever one falls on the question of plurality-majority versus proportional electoral systems, it is clear that the latter - used for example, in the Netherlands - is more representative of the people's votes than the former, as used in the UK.

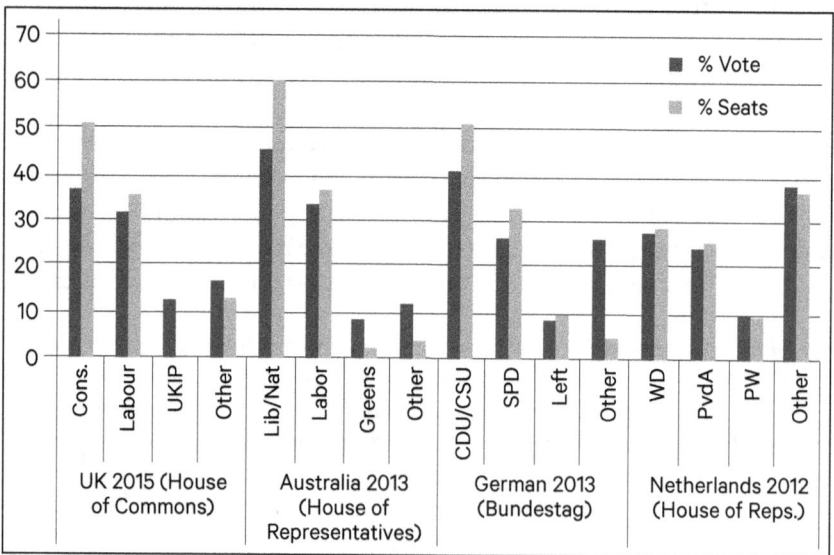

By comparing the third-placed parties in above graphic (UKIP in the UK, Greens in Australia, Left in Germany and PVV -Wilders in the Netherlands),

we can see why voters for minor parties in plurality-majority systems would feel discriminated against. The UK is an extreme example. UKIP received a third of the vote of the winning Conservatives, yet this translated into only one seat in parliament. Similarly, the Australian Greens vote of almost 10% resulted in only a single seat in their so-called House of Representatives - a clear indictment of the unrepresentativeness of the system.

The Netherlands on the other hand, has one of the purest forms of proportional representation in the world, with all the discrepancies being less than 1 percent. If a party earns 10 percent of the votes, they get 10 percent of the seats in parliament. The German system is a mix of two systems; however, the proportional element is deliberately used to correct the disproportionality of the plurality-majority part".

The idea of using citizens assemblies for the kind of major reforms discussed earlier in this text deserves consideration. As we shall see later, when referring to the work of the law academic Dr. Bede Harris in particular, deliberation about such matters is very necessary to increase people's knowledge about the options. Participation in such discussions about governance by randomly selected groups is quite rare in Australia but could have the same positive effect as it has had elsewhere. It could be empowering! What could be more enlightening than frequent face to face discussions about a new Constitution, the replacement of Federation by a less expensive, more effective system of decentralisation, e.g., resulting in cheaper housing options, amongst many other advantages.

Cheaper housing may be successfully offered by the many rural cities but needs to be accompanied with job creation in the regions, something that seems to have been abandoned for some 35 years now. Sadly, that is more or less the same period of time that we have been told by idealistic economists who preached that the market mechanism fixes everything. Clearly it often doesn't work like that. As a result of that neo-liberal ideology the big cities have grown rapidly while more and more people are encouraged to live in them in smaller and more expensive houses.

The author of this text lived and worked for 22 years in the Northern Rivers area of NSW (Lismore) and witnessed the dramatic effect of the tertiary educational institution that was established there in 1974, the Northern Rivers CAE, later to become Southern Cross University. This University brought employment, ideas and investment to the region. It had a galvanising impact through several faculties, including art, agriculture, sport, business, tourism, education and engineering. The university soon became the largest employer in the region. It contributed to many other changes in the Far North Coast of

NSW. Together with the strong influx of the Greens, first in Nimbin and later throughout the region, Northern NSW went through a revolution which had political consequences as well. Several state and federal seats became marginal, a sure condition to attract funding or promises for funding from major parties in the prevailing SMD electoral system.

Some of this was actually recommended and forecast by the progressive 1970s scholar Hugh Stretton. In *Ideas for Australian cities* (1970). He wrote "Line up and had for the bush", referring to the role of Colleges of Advanced Education in often out of the way places to generate or assist the growth of new cities. Southern Cross had that effect in Lismore and the region although regular floods in the city centre also helped to locate the construction of the new University well away from that centre.

We need to turn now to the constitutional issue that Section 44 presented Australia with in 2017.

Chapter 1

Section 44 and the decision of the High Court in retrospect. The disruption of Parliament and the consequences. The situation at the close of 2017.

Relevant sections of the Constitution read as follows:

42. Oath or affirmation of allegiance

Every senator and every member of the House of Representatives shall before taking his seat make and subscribe before the Governor-General, or some person authorised by him, an oath or affirmation of allegiance in the form set forth in the schedule to this Constitution.

44. Disqualification

Any person who:

1. is under any acknowledgment of allegiance, obedience, or adherence to a foreign power, or is a subject or a citizen or entitled to the rights or privileges of a subject or a citizen of a foreign power; or

2. is attainted of treason, or has been convicted and is under sentence, or subject to be sentenced, for any offence punishable under the law of the Commonwealth or of a State by imprisonment for one year or longer; or

3. is an undischarged bankrupt or insolvent; or

4. holds any office of profit under the Crown, or any pension payable during the pleasure of the Crown out of any of the revenues of the Commonwealth: or

5. has any direct or indirect pecuniary interest in any agreement with the Public Service of the Commonwealth otherwise than as a member

and in common with the other members of an incorporated company consisting of more than twenty-five persons;

shall be incapable of being chosen or of sitting as a senator or a member of the House of Representatives.

But subsection (iv) does not apply to the office of any of the Queen's Ministers of State for the Commonwealth, or of any of the Queen's Ministers for a State, or to the receipt of pay, half pay, or a pension, by any person as an officer or member of the Queen's navy or army, or to the receipt of pay as an officer or member of the naval or military forces of the Commonwealth by any person whose services are not wholly employed by the Commonwealth.

45. Vacancy on happening of disqualification

If a senator or member of the House of Representatives:

1. becomes subject to any of the disabilities mentioned in the last preceding section; or

2. takes the benefit, whether by assignment, composition, or otherwise, of any law relating to bankrupt or insolvent debtors; or

3. directly or indirectly takes or agrees to take any fee or honorarium for services rendered to the Commonwealth, or for services rendered in the Parliament to any person or State;

his place shall thereupon become vacant.

46. Penalty for sitting when disqualified

Until the Parliament otherwise provides, any person declared by this Constitution to be incapable of sitting as a senator or as a member of the House of Representatives shall, for every day on which he so sits, be liable to pay the sum of one hundred pounds to any person who sues for it in any court of competent jurisdiction.

Constitutional Law Professor Chery Saunders writes in her annotated *The Australian Constitution* (1997) "The High Court has held that Australians with dual citizenship are disqualified from running for Parliament unless they have taken all reasonable steps to abandon their non-Australian citizenship".

Naturally, in cases of doubt the question then arises: What are these "reasonable steps"? That is a matter for the High Court to establish apparently.

In 1901 an Australian citizenship did not exist at all. All citizens were British subjects. Anybody who wasn't British was a foreigner. The notion of Australian citizenship only came in with the Citizenship Act of 1948. It was later amended a number of times and is now known as the Australian Citizenship Act, 2007. In 1988 the High Court ruled that Britons would need to apply to be Australian citizens; that they were British subjects was no longer sufficient. They could then be "dual citizens" but, as such, could not be a member of the federal parliament. They would have to renounce British citizenship. Could anyone (of the several who were British subjects as well, mostly by descent) be a danger to Australia? This idea doesn't make sense.

There have been several other cases over the years where sitting members were challenged or disqualified on the basis of not only dual citizenship (1) but also for other reasons, especially "profit under the Crown". The author of this book stood as a candidate for the federal seat of Richmond in 1984 and had to forgo six weeks salary as an academic of the Northern Rivers CAE in Lismore (later Southern Cross University). The sense of that provision escaped me but I heard about this only after the pre-selection and it was then difficult to withdraw. It certainly was my loss because the seat was a safe seat of the National Party. Details of such cases can be found on the Internet in an e-Brief by Ian Holland of the Politics and Public Administration Group *(https://www.aph.gov.au/ About_Parliament/Parliamentary_Departments/Parliamentary_Library/ Publications_Archive/archive/Section44)*

The relevant aspect of a Parliamentary Report about Prominent Recent Cases is the growing awareness of the mounting problems of Section 44. The Standing Committee on Constitutional and Legal Affairs in its Report of 1981 (!) *The Constitutional Qualifications of Members of Parliament* recommended that every one of the five subsections of Section 44 be either amended or deleted, by referendum. Especially the Australian Democrats pushed for major changes but the important fact is that no referendum was held and NOTHING was changed.

On 29 October 1996 , following the High Court ruling in Free v Kelly, Greens' Senator Bob Brown also moved a motion calling on the Government to formulate a proposal for amendment of the Constitution to deal with Section 44. The motion was passed without a division, but no referendum was organized.

Two years later, there having been no further action on the House of Representatives Committee Report, Senator Bob Brown introduced a Bill into the Senate, titled the Constitutional Alteration (Right to Stand for Parliament Qualification of Members and Candidates) Bill 1998. Its intention was to alter both subsections 44(i) and 44(iv) of the Constitution. Senator Brown's Bill highlighted one of the problems with reforming Section 44. Everyone agreed that the Section is unsatisfactory. However, there were significant differences of opinion over how it should be changed. Senator Brown wanted to replace subsection 44(i) with a requirement that a candidate be an Australian citizen. During debate on the Bill on 3 December 1998, however, it was clear that others, such as National Party Senator Bill O'Chee, believed that a candidate should hold *only* Australian citizenship.

After the 1998 election, Senator Brown put the Bill back on the notice paper, and it was debated again on 15 May 2003. On this occasion, the Bill secured the support of the ALP Opposition, the Australian Democrats, Australian Progressive Alliance and the Greens, as well as independents Shane Murphy and Brian Harradine of Tasmania. However, a Bill proposing an amendment to the Constitution must pass each chamber by an absolute majority (see the Constitution, Section 128). When Senator Brown's Bill was put to the vote, it secured the majority of votes in the chamber, but fell short of an absolute majority by three votes. Had another three of the ALP Senators present on the day but absent from the chamber for the division, it is likely that the Bill would have passed the Senate. However, unless there was a change in the Government's view, it would have faced defeat in the House of Representatives.

On 30 October 2003, the Senate passed a motion moved by Australian Democrats Senator Andrew Bartlett, expressing the Senate s view that sections 44(i) and 44(iv.) of the Constitution should be amended to remove the current prohibition on dual citizens and public sector employees being able to nominate for election to the Commonwealth Parliament .

The same Ian Holland, as quoted above, wrote this in the *Sydney Morning Herald*, **14 years later** (20.7.2017):

Section 44 of Constitution must change after Larissa Waters, Scott Ludlam resign

"Early in the evening of August 23, 2011, I went into the Senate chamber, and sat on the deep red leather seats in the advisor's box. It was a special moment, listening to Larissa Waters, my former talented student in Brisbane, give her first speech as a Senator. She described herself having "determined optimism",

and that certainly was the student I remembered. With a broad Australian accent, she applied herself to contributing to Australian political life.

Now, thanks to the arcane workings of Section 44 of our Constitution, she is gone. Resigned because she mistakenly thought that, when your Australian parents carry you from a country at 11 months and never go back, and you are naturalised as an Australian, and have an Australian passport, and contribute for years to your country, you might just be Australian enough to hold office."

How did the issue of dual citizens ship protest become such a fiasco?

There are three main reasons:

1. The High Court decided to apply the Black Letter approach.

2. An inability to update the Constitution as shown above since 1981 – it didn't even reach the status of an official Referendum.

3. The unwillingness of the major parties to propose amendment proposals and tackle Constitutional renewal.

Re Canavan; Re Ludlam; Re Waters; Re Roberts [No 2]; Re Joyce; Re Nash; Re Xenophon (commonly referred to as the "Citizenship Seven case") is a set of cases, heard together by the High Court of Australia sitting as the Court of Disputed Returns, arising from doubts as to the eligibility of a number of members of Parliament to be elected to Parliament because of section 44(i) of the Constitution.

The Court unanimously held on 27 October 2017 that a dual citizen, irrespective of whether they knew about their citizenship status, will be disqualified from Parliament unless they have taken "all steps that are reasonably required" to renounce their other citizenship. The Court rejected arguments that would change the approach to section 44(i) of the Constitution, maintaining the approach of the majority in *Sykes v Cleary*.

Judgment

On 27 October 2017, the High Court handed down its decision. In a unanimous judgment, the Court interpreted s 44(i) according to the "ordinary and natural meaning" of its language. On that approach, it first affirmed the view taken in *Sykes v Cleary* that the question of eligibility is to be determined with reference to the point of nomination. The Court then followed the reasoning of the majority in *Sykes v Cleary*. The Court said in part (emphases added):

A person who, at the time that he or she nominates for election, retains the status of subject or citizen of a foreign power will be disqualified by reason of s 44(i), except where the operation of the foreign law is contrary to the constitutional imperative that an Australian citizen not be **irremediably prevented** by foreign law from participation in representative government. Where it can be demonstrated that the person has **taken all steps that are reasonably required** by the foreign law to renounce his or her citizenship and within his or her power, the constitutional imperative is engaged.

The Court ruled that the fact of citizenship was disqualifying, regardless of whether the person knew of the citizenship or engaged in any voluntary act of acquisition. It emphasised that to hold otherwise would introduce an element of subjectivity that **"would be inimical to the stability of representative government"**. It followed that each of Joyce, Ludlam, Nash, Roberts and Waters had been ineligible to be elected.

However, Canavan and Xenophon had been eligible. It was determined that Canavan, under Italian law, was not a citizen of Italy. It was found that Xenophon was a British Overseas citizen, but that this did not give him the right to enter or reside in the United Kingdom; therefore, for the purposes of s 44(i), he was neither a citizen nor entitled to the rights and privileges of a citizen of the United Kingdom. The Court declared the seats of the ineligible members to be vacant, It ordered that the vacancy in the House of Representatives be filled through a by-election and that the vacancies in the Senate be filled by "special counts" (ie, countbacks) of the ballot papers in each State, subject to supervision by a Justice of the Court.

We'll briefly consider each relevant aspect in a broader perspective than the High Court felt necessary. The High Court is of course entirely familiar with Section 44 and the problems of dual citizenship in the past, perhaps less so with the many others who would be or could now be affected by an adverse finding, in other words: the consequences. However, the decision was unanimous: Black Letter and precedent. The decision to stick to the 1901 law was in itself highly problematic. The law, as it stood was archaic and referred to an entirely different citizenship situation. This in itself provided a plausible and indeed possible reason for the High Court to refrain from the decision they made. However, instead they decided to act in the spirit of the Section (1): preventing a danger presented by dual citizenship – the additional citizenship that could possibly present danger to Australia.

Four points can be made in the first instance.

a. Looking at the first parliamentarians with dual citizenship (US, NZ, Italy, Greece, and the UK), there was no such danger to Australia at all, none whatsoever. In 1901 this had been the major justification, the clear intent of those who drafted the Constitution!

b. The "culprits" had no or scant knowledge of them having dual citizenship. While this may not be an excuse, the consequence of losing a job for the individual and their party, even the Government's survival of the day was serious. These people were elected in good faith. The voters would also be punished to turn up for a new election. Money of parties and the government had to be spent.

c. It was not possible to appeal the decision.

d. The High Court's argument that to rule otherwise **"would be inimical to the stability of representative government"** is highly debatable.

Many would say that the Court's decision actually threatened that.

In the late nineteenth century, many English-speaking countries, Dominions like Australia, were part of the British Empire. The reasonable objective was not to have people in the Parliament who were citizens of a country with which Australia possibly could have a significant conflict. However, rather than acknowledging that Section 44 (i) of the 1901 Constitution had that *practical* meaning, the High Court instead decided that it must be read literally. Surely, this doesn't make sense. It could even be argued that it deliberately avoids a difficult debate. This has already led to some strange situations. For instance, Senator Stephen Parry, President of the Senate, waited with outing himself, understandably, to see what the Court's ruling would be. His ineligibility was due to his father's UK citizenship. Apparently, as one commentator remarked, had it been his mother who had migrated from England, there would not have been an issue regarding eligibility.

Others have commented on this decision. Political Science Professor Don Aitkin, a former University Vice Chancellor, wrote:

"Faced with all of this, the High Court unanimously took a straightforward interpretation of the Constitution. We can't solve this mess for you, they said. You have to sort it out yourself. And that is not at all easy. My guess is that several dozen, possibly small hundreds, of former MPs and Senators have held their places quite illegally. None of the recent discovery is really new, however, for in 1988, 1992 and 1999 the Court overturned election in three cases where those in question were found to be dual citizens. The current ruling means that dual citizens must have taken 'all steps that are reasonably required' to renounce their other citizenship. And that can be difficult to do, for not every country allows you to do so, or makes such renunciation easy. What is 'reasonable', and to whom?

So, there will be a short-term band aid fix, and no one presently much wants to go further. But there is need to do so, in my opinion. It is surely worrying that another country can apparently determine whether or not one of our citizens is eligible to stand for our national parliament. I had hoped that the High Court might say something to this effect. And it did so, in what seems to me a stilted way:

'A person who, at the time that he or she nominates for election, retains the status of subject or citizen of a foreign power will be disqualified by reason of s 44(i), except where the operation of the foreign law is contrary to the constitutional imperative that an Australian citizen not be irremediably prevented by foreign law from participation in representative government. Where it can be demonstrated that the person has taken all steps that are reasonably required by the foreign law to renounce his or her citizenship and within his or her power, the constitutional imperative is engaged'.

What is the 'constitutional imperative'? My reading, for what it is worth, is that no other country can have the right to dictate whether or not an Australian citizen can stand for our national parliament. I take it to be an assumption, a sort of basic law: Australians decide their own rules, because we are an independent nation-state. Ergo, the fact that a Greek Australian who has never sought to be a Greek in Greece or to hold a Greek passport or in any other way to act as a Greek citizen, should not prevent such a citizen's offering himself or herself as a candidate in Australian federal elections."

Source: *"The dual citizenship scandal/imbroglio/fiasco"* On Line Opinion, 24 November, 2017

The High Court's reasoning is quite mysterious probably for many readers as well. Frankly, it might have been much wiser, even more courageous, and certainly more creative and pragmatic, to decline or reserve judgement. Alternatively, it could have decided that the Constitution had been breached but that the transgressors would be required to renounce their other citizenship within a limited period, say, six months. Although High Court referred it to the *Joint Standing Committee on Electoral Matters* (JSCEM) for further consideration on what to do in future, it failed to decide that the Constitution was inadequate to deal with this matter. The major parties dominate this committee. It has only made minor adjustments in the past.

Aitkin recommends the replacement of Section 44 but does not consider the wider context of the problems of amendment. The need to amend this particular Section has been stated by many, since 1981, but it is not happening. Why is this so? That is the broader and most essential issue. It is relevant to much of the dated Constitution.

The High Court decision seems to have been unwise. And also, bureaucratic, safe and conservative. It does not consider the possible consequences for the Parliament and the Government, or the cost to the nation. Remarkably, it was a *unanimous* decision. Not one of these intelligent and experienced judges, enjoying very high status in Australian society, appears to have had an inkling that this could be an incompetent and bad decision. It was also an opportunity lost to initiate reform. By publicly calling on the major parties to *jointly* campaign on Constitutional reform the High Court would have done much better.

This brings us to the more general issue of the role of senior judges: Do they simply apply the law or do they also have a role in making the law? In chapter 2 we will examine this question in some detail.

Who are the politicians affected by the end of December 2017?

The cost of the entire exercise by year's end and the results of two by-elections during which Deputy PM and Member of New England Barnaby Joyce and Bennelong MP John Alexander were re-elected was reportedly $11.6 million dollars. There may well be much more to come as several ALP MPs are also affected, contrary to earlier assurances.

By the end the first week in December it was clear that another five Labor MPs could possibly be dual citizens at the time of nominating as a candidate for election. This was contrary to what Mr. Shorten had claimed earlier that all had taken all reasonable steps to ensure that they were eligible to stand. Just what was reasonable was no doubt a matter of opinion. Clearly, the prospect of several more by-elections early in 2018 loomed quite large.

David Feeney, Emma Husar, Anne Aly and Katy Gallagher were uncertain about their status. Feeney said he had signed renunciation documents and sent them to relevant authorities in both Britain and Ireland but, apparently, he had never received confirmation that this was successful. Kathy Gallagher was most reluctant that her case was to be referred to the High Court but eventually agreed that this needed to be done. Her case was seen as a test case that would determine the future of three ALP backbenchers in the same situation: Justine Keay, Susan Lamb and Josh Wilson.

There were still other Coalition members who are in some doubt: Liberals Jason Falinsky, Alex Hawke, Nola Marino, Julia Banks and Anne Sudmalis. On 5th December, the ALP wanted to refer all its possible "dual citizens" together with the four Coalition MPs but the Government refused more referrals from its own side. A motion was submitted by the ALP to that effect but it was lost on the casting vote of the Speaker Tony Smith. However, the uncertainty about the Government MPs remained unresolved.

Associate Professor Gabrielle Appleby commented:

> *"The issue, it would seem, is no longer the uncertainty around whether a person is or is not disqualified. Because of the strictness of the High Court's interpretation, all potential parliamentarians are on notice to check thoroughly their citizenship status. Part of the referral to the committee is to investigate ways to "minimise the risk of candidates being in breach of Section 44". Rather, the more fundamental issue is now whether this is a desirable state of affairs given the large numbers of Australian citizens who are dual nationals, and who may not wish to renounce their citizenship to run for parliament. Thus, we as a nation stand to lose potential parliamentarians by excluding a pool of people that is likely to grow, not diminish. Further, there is another question as to whether Section 44, when interpreted in this way, is apt to achieve its purpose. The High Court accepted that the purpose of Section 44 was to ensure that MPs do not have a split allegiance or loyalty. Many might argue that this purpose is still an important one. Even if that is accepted, it would seem that denial of eligibility to a dual national is a particularly blunt instrument to achieve it. On the one hand, it captures many people who do not even know they are dual citizens. On the other hand, the relatively easy step (in most cases) of renouncement means that those people who do have a split allegiance, but who want to run for parliament, have only to fulfil these formalities to do so."*

The Conversation, 27 October 2017.

In Chapter 6 of this text the question of political inclusion of multicultural Australia receives specific consideration. This recommendation of the High Court could result in restricting political inclusion. The JSCEM's recommendations on electoral systems have generally been in the interest of the major parties represented on it.

Chapter 2

Observations concerning the judiciary and politics.
a. The different roles of judges and politicians
b. The special role of a Constitutional Court in a Federation
c. The Federation is also a costly relic of the past.

a. The different roles of judges and politicians

The English political science professor John Griffith, of the London School of Economics and Political Science, presented the arguments for creative law makers in his well-known controversial classic *The Politics of the Judiciary*, 1985 (third edition). It is very much a book concerned with the relationship between the judiciary and politics. Reflecting on courts and judges and their roles he wrote:

> *"Statute law itself cannot be a perfect instrument. A statute or one section of a statute may be made to deal with some particular subject – perhaps with immigration, or drugs, or housing or education – but a situation arises where doubt is cast on the meaning of the words of the statute. Does the situation fall within these words or not? ....The judges then must decide how to interpret the statute and by doing so define its meaning. Not only therefore do judges "make law" through the development of the common law. They also do so by this process of statutory interpretation" (Ch 1, p.15)*

Judges are appointed and politicians are elected. The appointment of judges, especially senior judges, is seen as mostly an impartial process based on relevant achievement criteria, appropriate legal educational qualifications and experience. The situation the UK is broadly relevant but the notion that the appointments of senior judges there are entirely politically neutral is not correct in Griffith's view. However, politicians are rarely appointed as judges of the highest court, similar to the situation in Australia, post WWII. Also, judges are not expected to participate in any way in the political process. Griffith elaborates on the independence of the judges:

> "Judicial independence means that judges are not dependent on governments in any ways which might influence them in coming to decisions in individual cases. Formally, this independence is preserved by their not being dismissible by the government of the day." (p. 29).

However, this does not mean that political pressures or biases don't exist in some cases. But, ideally, judges must be impartial and seen to be impartial, according to Griffith. This applies to all civil and criminal cases. In political cases the situation is more nuanced really. Especially the role of class in the UK, certainly in the past, played a part in court cases dealing with trade unions for instance. Judges were seen as biased on account of their class and education. Sexism is another aspect, not discussed actually. All judges in the Griffith book are men! The author also distinguishes between "neutrality" and "impartiality". This is explained as follows:

> "I have said that, traditionally, impartiality is thought of as part of a wider neutrality. Judges are seen essentially as arbiters in conflicts whether between individuals or between individuals, and the state – as having no position of their own, no policy even in the widest sense of that word. In denying such neutrality, I am not concerned merely to argue that judges, like other people, have no personal political convictions and, with more or less enthusiasm, privately support one or other of the political parties and may vote accordingly. That, no doubt, is true but political partisanship is not important. What matters is the function they perform and the role they perceive themselves as fulfilling in the political structure. Neither impartiality nor independence necessarily involves neutrality. Judges are part of the machinery of authority in the state and as such cannot avoid the making of political decisions. What is important to know is the basis on which these decisions are made." (p. 195)

The theme of Judicial creativity is taken up particularly in Part Three of the book. Although writing in the context of the British post-WWII setting, and an in many ways different governance structure as compared to Australia (see below), there are sociological and historical contact points that do make a summary relevant to our context. Griffith strongly supports the need for creativity. In a country where much law has originated from the Common Law this is not surprising.

Judges in the UK and in Australia have a collective view of the Public Interest, although Griffith argues it is the judicial conception of the Public Interest. In the UK that is closer to that of the Conservative Party than the Labour Party. Judges also do have a longer life than most Ministers. This is important to realise. They are not beholden to Ministers unlike public servants who owe loyalty to them. Nevertheless, the judiciary is very much part and parcel of a democracy. Without it the institutions and the legal framework could not be maintained as it should. Thus, for it to have a creative function, that is on occasion making law through interpretation or providing advice to the legislature, is reasonable, even logical and useful, and to be expected from an active, with-it judiciary.

> *"When a particular interpretation – for example of the Race Relations Act – is objected to, it is common for the interpretation to be defended on the ground that all the judges can do it to apply the law as made by Parliament and not to improve it. But if the statute is open to more than one interpretation then the judges are supposed to discover, by looking at the whole of the law on the matter, including the statute itself, what was the intention of Parliament and to interpret accordingly. At this point strong disagreement may arise, even within the court itself." (p. 181)*

and later, after considering several pronouncements of Law Lords following the letter of the law and why they did so, like "the real difficulty about judges making law":

> *"All this leads to the conclusion that, as one might expect, judges like the rest of us are not all of a piece, that they are liable to be swayed by emotional prejudices, that their 'inarticulate major premises' are strong and not only inarticulate but sometimes unknown to themselves. The judges seldom give the impression of strong silent men wedded only to a sanctified impartiality. They frequently appear – and speak – as men with weighty, even passionate, views of the nature of society and the content of law and of their partial responsibility for its future development" (p. 185)*

The Australian situation

What is the status of High Court judges in relation to politicians in Australia? Out of 100: 74 : 16 according to a recent Roy Morgan survey.

Roy Morgan Image of Professions Survey 2017: Health professionals continue domination with Nurses most highly regarded again; followed by Doctors and Pharmacists

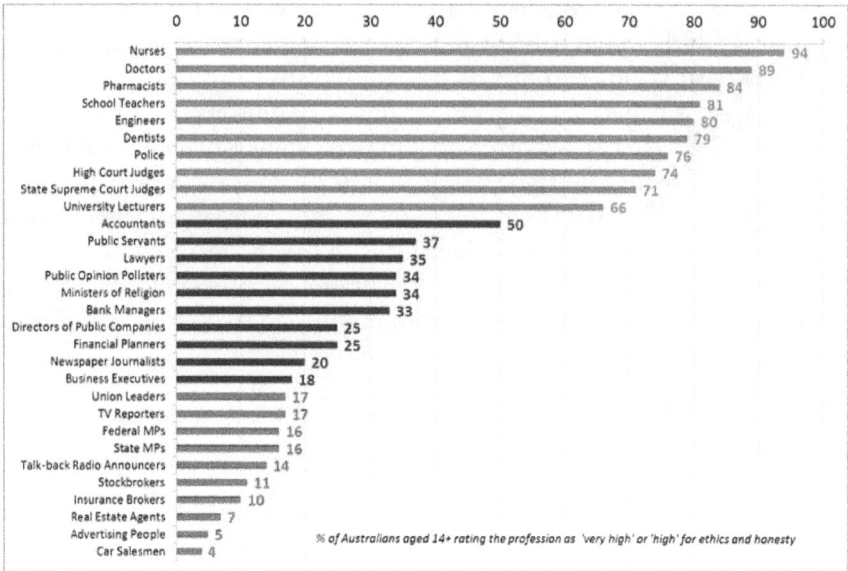

	0	10	20	30	40	50	60	70	80	90	100
Nurses											94
Doctors										89	
Pharmacists									84		
School Teachers									81		
Engineers									80		
Dentists									79		
Police								76			
High Court Judges								74			
State Supreme Court Judges							71				
University Lecturers							66				
Accountants					50						
Public Servants				37							
Lawyers				35							
Public Opinion Pollsters				34							
Ministers of Religion				34							
Bank Managers				33							
Directors of Public Companies			25								
Financial Planners			25								
Newspaper Journalists			20								
Business Executives		18									
Union Leaders		17									
TV Reporters		17									
Federal MPs		16									
State MPs		16									
Talk-back Radio Announcers		14									
Stockbrokers		11									
Insurance Brokers		10									
Real Estate Agents	7										
Advertising People	5										
Car Salesmen	4										

% of Australians aged 14+ rating the profession as 'very high' or 'high' for ethics and honesty

- June 07 2017
- Finding No. 7244

Health professionals have continued their domination of Australia's most highly regarded professions with 94% of Australians (up 2% from 2016) rating **Nurses** 'very high' or 'high' for their 'ethics and honesty'. **Nurses** have topped the annual survey for 23 years running since being included for the first time in 1994.Health professionals are clustered near the top with **Nurses** followed by **Doctors** on 89% (up 3%), **Pharmacists** on 84% (down 2%) and **Dentists** on 79% (up 4%). Only **School Teachers** on 81% (up 4%) and **Engineers** on 80% (up 2%) prevent a clean sweep at the top for health-related professionals.Of all 30 professions surveyed in 2017 sixteen decreased in regards to ethics and honesty while twelve professions increased and only two professions were unchanged according to the Roy Morgan survey conducted in the last week of May with 648 Australians.

Image of Professions 2017

Not all that much has been written in Australia about politics and the judiciary in Australia except in relation to federalism. In that respect former Chief Justice Sir Anthony Mason has pointed out that the power and scope of the Federal government has grown dramatically and has radically altered the federal balance by the Constitution, as compared to 1901. This even happened in spite of the fact that most constitutional amendment proposals favouring the growth of federal power were rejected and the two court cases soon after WWII, permitting the return of income tax powers to the states, were not acted on. However, these trends are not specifically what we are concerned about in this particular section. Nevertheless, the majority of appointments to the High Court tend to be judges with a conservative attitude, by social background, training and personal philosophy.

It has been obvious though that when vacancies occur on the High Court, and other Courts, political bias certainly does come into play after the technical and experience qualifications of the candidates have been fulfilled. A recent assessment by UNSW Law School Associate Professor and prolific AFR law journalist Gabrielle Appleby provides an excellent account:

"Late last week, the federal government appointed Geoffrey Nettle, a Victorian Court of Appeal judge, to the High Court to replace retiring justice Susan Crennan. Nettle is an excellent lawyer and his appointment was extremely well received. High Court judges have the final word on the interpretation of all laws across Australia. They have the final say on the interpretation of the constitutional limits within which the federal and state governments must operate. Understandably, then, the process and criteria by which these judges are selected are hotly contested. Australians will be best served by having exceptionally talented lawyers on the High Court. But should judges also be representative of the community that their rulings affect? What role should politics play in judicial appointments, if any?

The appointment process

The government has a pretty free hand in choosing High Court judges. To be eligible for a High Court appointment, a person must be – or have been – a judge of another court, or have been a legal practitioner for more than five years. Before a High Court appointment, there is a statutory requirement for the federal attorney-general to consult their state counterparts. However, the federal attorney-general doesn't have to act in accordance with any advice they may receive.

Nettle, the first of two High Court appointments the government will have to make in coming months, has been lauded for his exceptional legal mind, fairness and decency. After the fallout earlier this year over the Queensland government's appointment of Tim Carmody as Chief Justice of the state's Supreme Court, the federal government received high praise for avoiding a political appointment. Despite these deserved plaudits, Nettle is another white, male judge from the eastern states who was revealed to the Australian public as the fait accompli of a secret system.

The politics of High Court appointments

Under the current arrangements, the infiltration of politics into the High Court appointment process seems inevitable. On one view, it is even desirable. With very little accountability otherwise existing for judicial officeholders, the appointments process operates as an initial check on the courts. The government's discretion over appointments injects democratic legitimacy into the judicial process. In the US, Supreme Court judges are nominated by the executive and confirmed by the Senate, so both elected branches of government have input into the system.

In Australia, there has been surprisingly little recent concern over inappropriately "political" appointments, at least at the High Court level. Certainly, appointments of former politicians were common in the High Court's first decades. However, the High Court has not had a politician-judge since 1975, when Gough Whitlam's attorney-general, Lionel Murphy, was controversially appointed to the bench.

Today, it is usual for High Court judges to have had long and distinguished judicial careers before appointment, or occasionally to be appointed directly from practice.

Political influences have not been entirely removed from the process. Following the controversial native title decisions of Mabo v Queensland (No 2) and Wik Peoples v Queensland, former Nationals leader and deputy prime minister Tim Fischer remarked that increasing judicial activism demonstrated the need to appoint "capital-c" conservative judges to the bench.

Fischer believed that the judges were making decisions on the basis of political rather than legal considerations. If that's correct, it's understandable that a government may wish to appoint judges who share their politics. However, the introduction of overt political criteria into judicial selection has the capacity to undermine public confidence in the independence of the judiciary, causing enduring harm to the institution.

In the US, for example, the belief that the politics of individual Supreme Court judges influences their decisions – particularly in highly contested areas such as the right to abortion or the constitutionality of gun control – has turned Senate confirmation hearings into politically charged spectacles that do little for bolstering confidence in the integrity of the Supreme Court (or the Senate).

What does the ideal High Court judge look like?

In Australia, the lack of transparency is the most controversial aspect of judicial appointments. What criteria are applied? Who decides whether these criteria are met? It is pretty uncontroversial that merit must be the overriding criterion for judicial appointment. It creates a threshold that maintains confidence in the legal abilities of Australia's judicial officers. But selecting a single candidate from the top Australian judges and legal practitioners as the most meritorious is often impossible. They are all exceptional, so the merit principle needs to be supplemented.

There is an ongoing debate in Australia as to whether diversity, or representativeness, should also play a role in judicial selection. In 2012, the then attorney-general, Nicola Roxon, publicly attacked the lack of judicial diversity in Australia. She argued that it had the potential to affect the community's perception of the judiciary and their confidence in it. It has also been suggested that a diverse judiciary may bring different perspectives to how justice may be achieved. For example, Justice Bertha Wilson, Canada's first female Supreme Court judge, argued that men and women often conceive of legal problems differently. Men see problems as arising from competing rights, whereas women see problems as arising from competing obligations. Women therefore emphasise the importance of preserving relationships, not winning or losing. Do judges decide cases through the objective interpretation and application of the law, divorced from their personal values and experience? Legal realists argue that not only do judges make judicial choices based on personal values and experience, but that these choices are inherent in the judicial task. According to this view, the law often does not yield a single discernable answer, meaning that judges must make these choices. If such choices must be made, there is a strong argument that the personal characteristics of judges ought to reflect the diversity of the community they serve.

Reform in Australia a slow process

In 2008, following the lead of a number of states, then-attorney-general Robert McClelland introduced a more transparent, merits-based process for federal court appointments. The new system included a commitment to broader consultations, publishing selection criteria, advertising appointments and the creation of "advisory panels" to consider nominations and expressions of interest and develop a shortlist from which the attorney-general could make the final selection. All appointments were to be "based on merit". However, the government said it was also seeking to increase diversity in relation to gender, residential location, professional background and experience and cultural background. This new process did not apply to the High Court. At this level, McClelland committed only to consulting with a wider pool than the statutorily mandated state attorneys-general. He indicated he would also consult with current High Court justices and the state and territory chief justices.

McClelland's system represented a small step towards judicial appointments reform. But unlike similar reforms implemented in the UK, they were never formalised through legislation. On coming to office in 2013, the Abbott government abandoned them. Current Attorney-General George Brandis, without any notice, has returned to the secretive, government-dominated model. Even though the government has moved backwards on judicial appointments reform, excellent lawyers continue to be appointed to the High Court. Nobody would question that this is desirable, but is it enough?"

"Republished under Creative Commons" - ***Conversation***. December 9, 2014 (Dr. Appleby's contribution here is much appreciated, KW)

Additional note on basic UK laws: flexibility and decentralisation

We should realise that there is no written British Constitution as such. There are several basic laws which together form the "British Constitution", frequently referred to as "uncodified". There was until 1828 the Magna Carta (of 1215) to start with, but several clauses were repealed in that year. Below is a list that make up the United Kingdom's uncodified Constitution. We should also remember that the UK is NOT a federation, like Australia, that has (1) a written Constitution (of 1901) which divides the sovereignty of the nation between a federal government and the constituent units/states (with their own Constitutions), and (2) has a Constitutional Court that oversees and protects the federal Constitution.

Magna Carta 1215 — clauses 1, 9, and 29, as enumerated in 1297, remain in statute;(73) asserts the freedom of the English church, the liberties of the City of London among others, and establishes the right to due process.

Bill of Rights 1689 — asserts certain rights of Parliament and the individual, and limits the powers of the monarch;[74] the Parliament of Scotland passed the Claim of Right Act 1689

Crown and Parliament Recognition Act 1689 — confirms the succession to the throne and the validity of the laws passed by the Convention Parliament

Act of Settlement 1701 — settles the succession of the Crown; agreed by Scotland as part of the Treaty of Union

Acts of Union 1707 — union of England (which at the time included Wales) and Scotland

Acts of Union 1800 — union of Great Britain and Ireland

Parliament Acts 1911 and 1949 — asserts the supremacy of the House of Commons by limiting the legislation-blocking powers of the House of Lords

Life Peerages Act 1958 — establishes standards for the creation of life peers which gives the Prime Minister the power to change the composition of the House of Lords

Emergency Powers Act 1964 — provides power to employ members of the armed forces in work of national importance

European Communities Act 1972 — incorporates European law into UK law

House of Commons Disqualification Act 1975 — prohibits certain categories of people, such as judges, from becoming members of the House of Commons

Ministerial and Other Salaries Act 1975 — governs ministerial salaries

British Nationality Act 1981 — revises the basis of British nationality law

Senior Courts Act 1981 (originally Supreme Court Act 1981) — defines the structure of the Senior Courts (then called the Supreme Court) of England and Wales

Representation of the People Act 1983 — updates the British electoral process

Scotland Act 1998 — creates the Scottish Parliament and devolves certain powers to it

Government of Wales Act 1998 — creates the Welsh Assembly, devolves certain powers to it

Northern Ireland Act 1998 — creates the Northern Ireland Assembly and devolves certain powers to it

Human Rights Act 1998 — incorporates the European Convention on Human Rights into UK law

House of Lords Act 1999 — reforms the House of Lords removing most hereditary peers

Civil Contingencies Act 2004 — establishes a framework for national and local emergency planning and response

Since then, the following statues of a constitutional nature have become law:

Constitutional Reform Act 2005 — creates the Supreme Court of the United Kingdom and guarantees judicial independence

Constitutional Reform and Governance Act 2010 — reforms the Royal Prerogative and makes other significant changes

Fixed-term Parliaments Act 2011 — introduces fixed-term parliaments of 5 years

Succession to the Crown Act 2013 — alters the laws of succession to the British throne

Compared to the rigid structure of the Australian federation two benefits of the UK's de facto unitary state stand out: 1. there has been considerable flexibility; 2. a very high level of decentralisation has been achieved witness the status of Scotland, Wales, and Northern Ireland.

b. The special role of a Constitutional Court in a Federation

The late Australian Law Professor George Winterton, a strong supporter of a Republic for Australia, has written about the need for a new Constitution for Australia first in *"We the People"* (1994). His approach was to delete what, in his view, would no longer be required. Chapter 1 in that book presents the entire existing Constitution with a lot of material crossed out. It is one way to get one's message across but there are at least three problems with this approach. 1. It is not a complete rewrite at all; it is the old Constitution minus what is no longer required, old furniture that clutters up the place. 2. One is still left with the federal structure something that made sense in the late 1890s but is now actually a major, costly hindrance for Australia to progress. 3. The country would also be left with a Parliamentary Executive, essentially the Westminster system. There are also MAJOR other problems with that, explained later. In Chapter 2 Winterton discusses the **Form of government** that Australia could consider and, regrettably, presents then only the two options that many Anglo-Celtic Australian commentators seem to be limited to: the US Presidential system, and the Westminster system. If we are to seriously discuss a new Constitution for Australia we need to understand that the options are much wider and much more appropriate than that. He wrote:

> *"The possible forms of republican government are virtually limitless but most of the worlds republics adopt either the executive presidency, of which the archetype is the United States, or the parliamentary executive, which is essentially the "Westminster" system of responsible Government with a largely ceremonial elected President as head of state instead of a hereditary monarch. There are also several republics which combine features of both system, notably France." (p. 40)*

This is quite incomplete really. It is essential that a further explanation is provided here. Australian scholars tend to operate in an Anglo-centric arena of study. When they "go overseas" to gain higher degrees and "international" experience they usually end up in the UK, US, Canada, Ireland, New Zealand, perhaps earlier in Southern Africa, in other words English-speaking countries. A few will travel in other countries, perhaps even quite a few, but mostly as tourists, not as post-graduate students. What is particularly missing in the above characterisation of options – essentially just two – is all those countries that have extra-parliamentary executives meaning Governments that are outside the legislature and are not like the United States Presidential system. That includes basically most of the European countries. The other point that should be made is that the US system is very unique not only because it sets an example for a federal structure – after 1787 - but even more because it developed a very strong Presidency. That example has remained quite unique even though it has been a model for some Latin American Republics – although not very successfully. So, the two options listed by Winterton are quite insufficient as models for a new Australian Constitution. What exists in other countries, both Republics AND constitutional monarchies is actually far more important for Australia but many Australian scholars are not familiar with them. If anything, it may be regarded by the intellectual elites as of little relevance. In a multicultural society such an attitude is not helpful.

To begin with there are very few real federations, a dozen perhaps, including newly independent Republics. The idea of separation of powers between legislature, executive and judiciary is not typical of a federation as may seem from the two-model option. It was the French philosopher Baron de Montesquieu, who advocated this in the 18th century, a model that was followed in most European, extra-parliamentary systems but not in the UK. In the Westminster system the Government Ministers are elected MPs and the Alternative Government (the Opposition), also have to be Members of that Parliament. Thus Government and Opposition dominate the Parliament to a large degree. That is not the case in the US at all, and also not in many European countries. Even the US President is only in the House of Representatives on rare, specific occasions. However, several other federations don't have that strict separation of powers, e.g. Germany and Switzerland. A further difference is of course that there are still a lot of constitutional monarchies as distinct from Republics. The strongest advocate of a parliamentary executive was the conservative MP for Bristol, Edmond Burke, quite the opposite number of the French radicals and French revolution around 1789. In order to be a Minister one has to be an elected MP in the Westminster system. One of the problems associated with that is that the pool to select functionally competent Ministers from is small. In the UK it is about 600 minus the Opposition members but in a country like Australia it is 150 minus the Opposition numbers. In all state parliaments it is even well below that, think of Tasmania for instance. The obvious result of that is lack of functional competence in their portfolios. In extra–parliamentary systems the choice is almost infinitely larger. Anybody in the country willing and capable to serve in the Ministry can be selected. They don't even have to be a member of a particular party. Australia is in urgent need of greater competence.

There is of course an additional factor that is part and parcel of the two models mentioned by Winterton. That is the single-member-districts (SMD) used both in Westminster AND the US. This started off as First-past-the post and it is still used in the UK and US but was adapted and improved somewhat in Australia to include preferences (compulsory) for lower houses. In Tasmania the Hare-Clark proportional system was introduced in 1907 for their lower house and Hare-Clark proportional system was also introduced for the Australian Senate in 1949, and some other Upper Houses, and later for the ACT. (Hare-Clark PR is often also called Single Transferable Vote - STV).

In 1984 the electoral system for the Senate was changed to overcome the problems with compulsory preferencing by introducing "above the line" and "under the line" options which resulted in around 90% of the voters avoiding preferencing under the line and simply voting above the line for their preferred party. The cumbersome (compulsory) preferencing required with the Hare-Clark system was regularly abused by deal makers. Horse trading beyond closed doors followed to comply with the legislation by means of Group Voting Tickets. This very complex system was gamed so that the outcomes made the representation of the actual strength of the parties in the Senate quite problematical for the Government in power. A rather hurried reform, early in 2016, aimed primarily to end the gaming, was only partly effective so that it was still possible for several candidates with a tiny first preference vote to be elected. Nevertheless, several minor parties managed to gain representation in the Senate and it could even be said that, really ever since 1949, the Senate was often more representative of the people than the Government of the day. Some ideologically "centrist" parties did gain representation in the Senate and had a moderating effect at times.

Add to this that Senators are elected for six years and only half of them are up for election every three years. Furthermore, each state is represented by an equal number of Senators (a federal constitutional requirement). As there are huge and growing differences in population numbers among states distortions in representation are obvious. Federation became possible on the condition that the states would have this sense of equality expressed in the states' house of Parliament – in the same way as the US Constitution provides for equal representation of Senators in the US Senate. Nevertheless, the dominance of the two-party system in Australia, mostly also extended to the Senate. This is still the case but could change. Smaller parties favouring constitutional change are a possible pathway to a new Constitution. Before dealing with the role of the High Court and the great difficulty of amending and thus updating the Australian Constitution let me quote what my former colleague Richard Lucy wrote about Australia's political system in 1985:

"The Australian form of Government is characterised by an inclusive struggle between two systems of Government – responsible party government and a system which divides power between a number of governmental institutions.... We have a perpetually double-dealing struggle between the identities conferred by the governmental institutions and the identities by the parties. We have a complicated inextricably tangled mess – the full catastrophe called Australian politics" (The Australian Form of Government, 1985)

The federal structure of Government was particularly advocated by Andrew Inglish Clark, a very reformist Chief Justice of Tasmania, also Vice Chancellor of the newly established University there and strong campaigner for federation, much inspired as he was by the US example. Clark was involved in the several conferences for unification of the six colonies during the 1890s and was responsible for the text of 89 out of 128 sections of the 1901 Constitution. The political leaders, especially of NSW and South Australia, carried the day in the final conferences when federation was combined with the Westminster system, not Clark's preference apparently. Of course, we need to realise that this was a Federation unlike the US in that it was a colonial Federation enacted by an Act of British Parliament, quite unlike the US experience 100 years earlier. They rebelled against the British Imperial Government and won the battle in 1776. Nevertheless, Australia adopted the federal structure whereby the Constitutions of the six states remained in place and valid to a large extent. The Federal Constitution provided for a strict division of federal and state powers, enumerated in Section 51, the very essence of a true federation.

A High Court was also established which had two functions: (1) A final court of appeal for all lower courts (2) A Constitutional Court to uphold the division of powers between federal and state governments and anything to do with typically federal issues.

All federations have such a Court that has the specific function to maintain the federal constitutional organisation and powers. As a non-federation, essentially a unitary state, the UK does not have such a Court.

The term "federation" is often incorrectly applied to a situation where provincial governments have considerable functions and powers in what is in fact a unitary state.

c. The Australian Federation is also a costly relic of the past

Replacing federation - aiming at real decentralization

In recent years a number of former politicians have condemned the continuation of federation for very good reasons. However, at the same time, others and some change-resistant scholars have argued that federalism still has something to offer and that the problems are either imagined and/or insignificant. Therefore, they claim, federalism can be 'modernized', 'repaired', 'saved', 'rescued' or 'made to work'. In a 2012 text edited by Kildea, Lynch and Williams various arguments are put forward to show how 'practical' reforms may be achieved. The title *"Tomorrow's Federation"* suggests that they expect Federation to continue but its major problems may be overcome by more pragmatic piecemeal tinkering. This looks very much like capitulation; it suggests that many of the authors believe that major constitutional change is simply not possible. This book was the outcome of a $215.000 Government research grant. The book you are reading now is self-funded and self-published. It puts forward the notion that Federation has to go, the sooner the better, and be replaced by superior governance structures. Furthermore, that Australian society has the capacity to bring this about. Thirdly, that we should stop spending money on maintaining the status quo.

A spectacular number of federal-state money wasting and looming crises have emerged in federal Australia. They have rumbled on in major and minor public policy areas in recent decades, health services being possibly the most spectacular, transport difficulties and energy generation in the face of climate change not far behind. This situation, thankfully, has prompted considerable research about alternatives and public attitudes, amongst others by specialists at Griffith University. However, what we definitely do not need is the creation of still more states as is theoretically possible within the current Constitution. This would simply multiply the already troublesome duplications, political altercations and boost the number of state public servants in the process. The Ph. D thesis by Mark Drummond (2008) provided convincing evidence that the existing federal government has become extremely costly and is broken. Overall, the results demonstrate that there is much dissatisfaction amongst the general public with federal-state relations as well. Also, in contrast, a number of research papers with conservative messages have appeared, such as the work by Anne Twomey and Glenn Withers (2007), which aim to show that some other federations are doing well and that there is no cause for alarm here either. Ten years later we know of course that the Global Financial Crisis then started in the US, the first modern example of a federation. It spread from there, and that was not the first international catastrophe to emanate from the USA in the last decade. However, economic problems in a nation can of course have many other causes than the federal structure. Their work was perhaps commissioned by the then ALP State Premiers who, at that time, apparently felt sympathetic towards such an outcome, possibly after a study visit to Canada, which impressed them. Drummond later also analysed some of the outcomes of the *Australian 2020 Summit,* convened by Prime Minister Kevin Rudd in his first term. He found that of 790 people who entered submissions to the Governance stream, about 343 contained content that were highly critical of federal government, including about 134 that either explicitly called for the abolition of state governments or called for reforms very close to abolition. However, in contrast, a conference *Making Federalism Work* (ANSZOG 11/12 Sept, 2008) was mainly about that, rescuing federation. A subsequent Conference in Tenterfield, in October 2008, organized by the Federation Research Centre of Griffith University and the Institute of Public Administration Australia (IPAA) was considering "Cooperative Federalism". It was attended by many senior public servants, politicians and some academics. My own paper there *'Meliorist piecemeal tinkering with federalism: recipe for disaster?'* offered the view that Cooperative Federalism was no long-term solution for the problem of deteriorating federal-state relations at all. It startled many of the public servants present. The vested interest of especially state employed public servants is readily understood of course. Any major change, like replacing federation naturally requires a sensible transition of the activities of public servants without the loss of benefits of current employees.

A later paper by the late Richard Murray may seem to have been a new departure. It is entitled: *New Federation with a Cities and Regional Approach (2012).*

Murray was a retired senior economist of Treasury, with experience in the IMF. Much of his paper is devoted to improving fiscal imbalance, as have others done before him, e.g. the economist J. Pincus (*Six myths of federal-state financial relations,* CEDA 2007). The Murray proposal has some merit and is more progressive than the one by Pincus who judged the Australian federation as *"the most successful in modern history"*, a view that is difficult to match with reality. Even if it could be argued that federation was successful until perhaps WWII, since 1945 its usefulness has steadily declined and alternative structures could well be significantly superior.

Amazingly, what is altogether missing in the papers of Murray and Pincus is a discussion about what the essential characteristics of a federation are, why it is formed, and how the circumstances of the society it serves can change significantly over time. This can be so drastic that maintaining a once useful structure becomes a costly burden. A federation always requires a written constitution and a constitutional court overseeing the division of sovereignty laid down in that constitution. This has been so difficult in Australia that several well-known commentators have described the Constitution as 'frozen'. To get it out of the deep freeze, piecemeal tinkering and meliorism strategies are certain to fail. Yet, it seems extremely difficult to exit this mode of operation. Economists and constitutional lawyers approach federalism from a different perspective than political scientists. Federation is essentially a power bargain that is then written up in a constitution. The power relationships change over time, for all kinds of reasons, but the governments structures need to adapt. The vested interests to block that are strong but the time has come for major changes.

Galaxy Public Opinion Poll

In February 2013 and in May 2014 the **Beyond Federation** group engaged a reputable Opinion Pollster (Gallaxy) to test public opinion. In the first test, it presented one particular question to a national sample of 1052 Australians aged 18 years and over:

Question:

Thinking now about state and federal laws. Currently there are different laws in the eight states and territories of Australia. Would you be in favour or opposed to having just one set of laws for the whole country?

Three answers were possible: 1. In favour: 2. Opposed: 3. Neither/Don't know.

Main Findings

* The majority of Australians are in favour of having a unified set of laws for all states and territories. Overall, 78% are in favour of having one set of laws, 19% are opposed and 3% are uncommitted.

* This means that those in favour of a single set of laws outnumber those opposed by a factor of four to one.

* Majority support may be observed across all key demographic groups and all states of Australia.

In May 2014 the Gallaxy pollsters put the following questions to a national sample of 1050 people, 18 years and over.

It has been estimated that the abolition of State governments could benefit Australia to the tune of at least $40 billion per annum. If a referendum were held on the question of whether State governments should be abolished, would you support the abolition of State governments?

Yes 1,   No 2, Don't know 3.

Main Findings

1. Opinion is divided on whether the State governments should be abolished. While 39% of the population think they should be, 31% are opposed and 30% undecided.

2. Although those in favour of abolishing State governments outnumber those opposed, the large number of those undecided and the tendency for voters to prefer to maintain the status quo means that a referendum on the issue would be unlikely to be carried at the present point in time.

3. Those aged 50 years and older (50%) are the most likely to be in favour of the abolition of State governments. In contrast, only 18% of those aged 18-24 years see a need to abolish State governments, with the majority of these young voters (51%) undecided.

4. Men (46%) are more likely than women (32%) to support the abolition of State governments.

5. These results confirm the need for an education campaign, if the push for the abolition of State governments is to be successful. Key targets for the campaign will include young voters and women.

The historical development of federalism – and its decline – has been predicted correctly by eminent Australian commentators as early as 1902 when Alfred Deakin, the second prime minister, said that the *"Commonwealth would increase in stature, in financial dominance, and in the determination of national priorities"*. Professor Gordon Greenwood (1942) later wrote that

"Despite its achievements, the evidence points decisively to the conclusion that the federal system has outlived its usefulness, that the conditions which made federation a necessary stage in the evolution of Australian nationhood have

largely passed away, and that the retention of the system now operates only as an obstacle to effective government and to a further advance."

At present the Australian Constitution, as well as the political system, is frozen. Sawer already remarked on this 51 years ago (Sawer, 1967). The refrain of 'cooperative federalism' is like hearing an old gramophone record with the needle stuck in the groove.

Twomey and Withers (2007) briefly considered the alternative of abolishing the states and replacing them with a much larger number of regions, but rejected that as *"impractical and costly"*. They gave no consideration to a decentralised unitary model comprising a new national government and stronger local governments, including (metropolitan) city governments. Existing regional organisation of councils could play a more significant role in assisting local government, facilitating improved subsidiarity. There are already 64 in place in Australia, some of them providing excellent services to local governments (e.g. Western Sydney Organisation of Councils, WSROC). Also ignored are problems with the electoral systems, the resulting archaic two-party system and the extremely rigid and now ossified Constitution itself. The Business Council of Australia has issued at least two major reports on Federal-State complexities and inefficiencies, e.g. the high number of taxes impacting on business. They estimated the cost of federation to be approximately $9 billion a year (BCA, 2006). Still, the BCA also favours 'cooperative (seamless) federalism'. Federalism without boundaries? A ridiculous idea which suggests a complete lack of understanding why federations are formed – and why they disappear. Are they suggesting that the clock should be turned back? Did they look further than business interests?

Perhaps the most questionable conservative defence is that "a unitary state equals centralization of power". This almost sounds like a remnant of cold war thinking. Surprisingly, the economist Pincus nevertheless pointed approvingly to France, which is politically highly centralized but administratively effectively decentralized. There are many other examples, which demonstrate that unitary states are often actually more decentralized than federal Australia. Drummond initially put the cost of continued federation at around $30 billion per annum (in 2008). Most estimates vary from $ 9 billion to $40 billion. It could easily be much more simply because future savings are often difficult to quantify. How can one express in dollar terms progress of a national system that is effectively decentralized in which regions and country towns suddenly start to flourish as never before?

Former Prime Minister Bob Hawke called for the abolition of states, at the Woodford Festival in December 2013 and, again, in December 2015

In 2013 he actually called for a new model of federalism that dumped the states in favour of a system of centralised government that would "immensely" strengthen the democratic process. He said:

> *"I made this proposition once that the states were quite artificial creations that were just represented lines on a map, there was no intrinsic merit in that at all."*

Actually, Hawke used the term "federalism" then in a way that is not federalism in a strictly legal sense - built on the shared constitutional sovereignty as with the current federation. It is actually a unitary state he has in mind with strong regions built on meaningful regional qualities - of which there can be many.

Source: http://www.couriermail.com.au/news/bob-hawke-calls-for-abolition-of-states-in-speech-at-woodford-folk-festival/news-story/fda6b5c4e2497fa612eaf7d0361e70f5

In December 2015 Hawke raised the issue again and even more determined. It can be accessed in full here at this URL:

http://www.smh.com.au/federal-politics/political-news/bob-hawke-says-abolish-state-governments-and-think-big-to-fix-the-nation-20161228-gtiwgv.html.

It was also Bob Hawke who in a Boyer lecture (1979) argued that the Westminster system prevented people from outside the Parliament to become Ministers, repeated at the 1992 APSA Conference where he was a guest during the special Republic discussion day. Just how long will it take Australian politicians to accept these straightforward sensible recommendations from senior politicians??

The Reform the Federation Inquiry 2014/2015

This inquiry was instigated by the Abbott government and driven by two former ALP Premiers the late John Bannon and John Brumby.

The Reform of Federation Inquiry was a failure, as much as the Abbott Government was a failure. To think that the huge imbalances in federal-state financial relations can be reversed even to a pre-1942 situation is to ignore history and common sense. Some of those who want to turn the clock back under the motto that they want to improve, repair or rescue the federation were also insisting that COAG should be written into Australia's archaic Constitution, thereby further strengthening the federal structure.

Piecemeal tinkering with the existing federation cannot make it work or make the patient better, to the contrary. The underlying problems remain and grow worse. One of the crucial aspects of the current federal system is that the state governments' principal occupations, activities and expenditures are concentrated on the major cities rather than the rural and regional areas of their states. As a result decentralisation has fallen by the wayside almost completely. State Governments are increasingly just city governments. That is especially the case in the Eastern States, particularly NSW and Victoria. Why not have city governments for the larger cities as part of the second tier of government in a new Constitution. The national government can then actively take care of regional and local government everywhere. The neglect of decentralisation and the development of huge areas of Australia that are now operating in the shadow of the major cities would end.

Our first port of call would be to address the apparently impossible situation that the Constitution "cannot" be amended to suit the nation as it is now and how it should be shaped for the future. **Why is this so?** That question is rarely raised in Australia, not by the major parties, not by academics and not by the Public Broadcasters either, especially the ABC which clearly has an educational role here that they do NOT adequately discharge. However, we should look well beyond the serious inadequacies of Section 128. The case for rewriting the entire Constitution is as strong as for replacing federation.

Secondly, the problems with Australia's electoral systems are also enormous. Some people fail to see the relevance of them to constitutional change. They are very relevant. The compulsory preferential single-member-district (SMD) system has given Australia an absolutely dysfunctional adversarial two-party system since well before WWII. This system blocks the generation of constitutional amendments; or, if generated, the passing of them in referendums. The federal-state differences are further aggravated by having different parties in government in Canberra and in the states. The blame game, already a highly negative feature of the party system in lower houses, is intensified enormously by federal-state differences. Of course, there are remedies for all this but the major parties are not interested in them or are incapable of generating them. In addition, we should realise that our Parliaments are not at all fully representative of the population.

The factional character of the major parties blocks flexibility in the Parliaments. There are several major issues that could generate cross party support but the major party rigidity prevents alignments that would be helpful for progress. The concentration of the Turnbull Government on "Jobs and Growth" completely ignores these major governance system obstacles. By the end of 2017 the Turnbull Government has very little to show in terms of achievements. The right wing of the Coalition parties has made a middle of the road policy agenda almost totally impossible. Turnbull's standing in the polls is as bad as Abbott's when he was replaced. He would need to embark on very different policy direction to be re-elected in 2019. At the time of writing this seems highly unlikely.

Given that far-reaching budgetary stresses have emerged in Australia, as a result of several hard to combat factors, the cost of federation as a structure, possibly $40 to $50 billion per annum, has now become of paramount importance. However, it is not just the cash expense. The Beyond Federation's Facebook page has demonstrated delays, the mistakes by state governments, the unproductive adversarialism inherent in the party system, aggravated by the federal structure. In spite of this malaise neither major party considers its replacement and the abolition of the states. What is so sacrosanct about this archaic Constitution?

Thirdly, the right to initiate constitutional referendums should be given to the people (CIR). At present only politicians can initiate proposals, in practice, only major party politicians. The fears that have been expressed about such a reform are completely unfounded. The fact that CIR is advocated by some people who have short-sighted policy objectives should not detract from the plainly democratic value of such a right.

Fourthly, certain aspects of the Westminster system, in particular that Ministers need to be "in and of the Parliament", actually destroy the separation of powers principle. The continual presence of the Government and Opposition executive in the Parliament (that is the House of Representatives and state lower houses), indeed the almost complete domination by them of the legislature, reinforces the polarised nature of the system. Australia needs to get away from that if agreement is to be reached about changing the system as it is. This fusion is undesirable. Not only is this a problem flowing from that ground rule, the Ministers are frequently functional amateurs because the choice of competencies is extremely limited indeed!

Holding on to Federation, as was the underlying objective of the Inquiry, was and is an undesirable, backward looking strategy. But quite apart from that the renewal of the Australian Constitution is very essential for many other reasons. One such reason is that we need much better system of decentralization and de-concentration of population in our five major cities. The poor use of living space in Australia and the growing traffic congestion in major cities is plainly ridiculous. It has much to do with the concentration of population in those cities and the failure of the states to decentralize. For Sydney to have over 6 m. people in 2036 is a monument to that failure, as is, of course, the absolutely parlous state of local government, the Cinderella of the system. That aspect, the need for effective decentralisation, has been accepted as a positive by the Turnbull government.

A new productive model would be a two-tier system, national and local government with mezzanine type regional councils representing kindred clusters of local governments. Already we have several examples of Regional Organisation of Councils on a voluntary basis. This is what needs constitutional recognition and coordination and for that purpose a COAG *could* serve a PROGRESSIVE FUNCTION rather than a reactionary purpose: Prepare the way for a new Constitution!

It would also make perfect sense to spread the Australian population to the many smaller towns and the rural areas for security reasons. The ridiculous urbanisation that has developed since 1945 in this huge continent is directly related to federalism. All those who argue that federation has served us well but that it is just in need of renovation are seriously in error. In many ways federation has not served Australian well at all ever since WWII. That the economy is ticking over in spite of the high cost of federation is due to many other favourable factors, e.g. existence of rich resources, a good climate, a highly motivated migrant work force, good education systems, good health provisions, scientific achievements and multicultural energies.

On the ***Beyond Federation*** Facebook page over 100 referrals to critical articles about continued federation have been posted - together with our introductory commentary (www.facebook.com/beyondfederation/). This page started in May 2015. We may publish these articles and our commentary in a small book if we can find financial support for that. It is a convincing tale of troubled relationships, confrontation between states and the national government over many policy issues and implementation. It'll convince the reader that major change is necessary.

Chapter 3

a. The promise of the Statute of Westminster 1931 and its adoption Act 1942.

b. The aftermath of the 1975 crisis: commentary YES, action NO.

a. The promise of the Statute of Westminster 1931 and its adoption Act 1942

Geoffrey Robertson (2013) has written a scathing assessment of 1901 in *Dreaming too loud*. It is interesting to consider the progress or otherwise since 1901:

> *"If I am a refugee from anything, it is from the Australian constitution, or at least from having to spend my time in court in arid argument over a constitutional law that is mainly about allocation of power between federal and state governments. Australians – or at least the Australian – react with mindless patriotism whenever 'our constitution' is said to need updating. It is necessary to remind them, in this case in a Bulletin edition celebrating in 2001 the centenary of Federation, of the virulence of the racism of the time, which ensured that human rights were absent from a document agreed at a referendum from which women, Blacks and territorians were excluded. It is anachronistic to see the Australian constitution in any true sense as the work of Australians: it was the work, more accurately, of unevolved Australians, who were hooked intravenously to British blood. And in the class-calcified Britain of Queen Victoria, where small children were put up chimneys and down mines, there was no talk of human rights."*

To the question "when did Australia become an Independent nation?" he gave seven answers in his 2009 book *The Statute of Liberty*. This is the list (restated in 2013):

1901: the year of federation, but this was far from real independence.

1931: The Statute of Westminster, another Act of Parliament following the "Balfour Declaration"

1939: that Statute of Westminster Adoption Act, passed in 1942 by the Australian Parliament, backdated to September 1939, on which day the Australian government felt itself bound by the British declaration of war on Germany.

1941: Declaration of War on Japan. The Curtin Government acted on its own initiative.

1942 : The Act removed doubts about the validity of Australian laws, but it did not apply to the states.

The Australia Acts, 1986 – seven laws enacted by the states, the British Government and finally by the Commonwealth government severed the constitutional tie to Britain. However, the British monarch remained as Australia's head of state, the Queen of Australia.

So, independent? "Not yet", Robertson claims, "because the constitution remains part of British law. The British Parliament's 'The Commonwealth of Australia Constitution Act 1900', although the source of federal power, is now the Australian Constitution, which can pursuant to Section 128 be amended or replaced by the Australian people voting in a referendum."

So, Robertson wrote,

> **"Until Australia decides to adopt a brand-new constitution, or at least amends the present document to establish a Republic, the source of federal power remains the UK parliament."**

In the 1890s the six colonies had a good deal of colonial autonomy some of which they surrendered to a federal government in 1901 for the sake of unity of purpose, and promoting inter-state trade and security. However, 117 years later this state autonomy has been steadily eroded. We now hear several politics professors saying that

> *"Australia is no longer a true federation because the states have lost their true sovereignty" (Wiltshire, 2008).*

Former WA Premier Carmen Lawrence, at a Constitution Day (9th July), organized by the ABC in Canberra in 2010, claimed that:

> *"The Australian community seems increasingly to hold the view that the states in their current form do not perform a useful role and the Federation requires a major overhaul."*

b. The aftermath of the 1975 crisis: commentary YES, action NO

Regardless of this evolutionary progress towards full independence from the UK serious governance system problems emerged in Australia. The written Constitution could hardly be amended, the electoral system has produced an ineffectual, adversarial two-party system and the competence of politicians is widely questioned. The Westminster baggage may appeal to part the conservative segment of the population still reflective of the Anglo-Celtic cultural norms but much less so to others. Voters have expressed growing dissatisfaction with the workings of the party system, the federation and the quality of leadership. Still, the power of these voters has actually weakened further over time. Many find they have to vote for the least objectionable major party, or face a fine. Remedies exist but who will initiate the debate for reform? Governance system innovation still seems foreign to most. Why is this so? This chapter seeks to find answers to such questions.

As a retired Associate Professor, who taught with Donald Horne at UNSW in the early 1970s (as a Tutor), I have written about possible alternatives in academic papers but the traditional media are only very rarely interested. There still appears to be a strong cultural bias in favour of the existing systems not only among politicians but also among academics and journalists. Consequently, their students, including journalists and editors, shy away from venturing outside the square. However, social media have moved away from this trend. *Independent Australia, On Line Opinion* and *Open Forum* are just three such examples. In addition, several new minor parties registered for the 2016 Double Dissolution to try their luck for a Senate seat - more than 50 in fact - were a clear expression of a desire for change. One of them, Vote/Flux, lamenting that representative democracy has become corrupted world-wide, wants to renew democracy, to be "Issue-based-Direct Democracy". The idea of Citizen Assemblies is given limited support by them. There were several others with more limited objectives but clearly inspired by the disenchantment of the current political system as not providing an adequate democratic outcome.

It would be fair to say however that the popular disenchantment with today's political class is less directed at the politicians as representatives than at the system of which they are the performing members. A minority of major party politicians can see the system flaws very clearly and would, very likely, accommodate system change and adjust quickly. E.g. the outmoded idea that the ALP can only rule "in their own right" is extra-ordinarily archaic and not practised in the many countries with multi-party districts and parliaments, including, for instance, New Zealand!

However, most of the political **leaders** demonstrate no inclination to tackle governance issues. Former PM Rudd concentrated essentially on applying Keynes' economics during the Global Financial Crisis. During an election campaign, he did propose a kind of tripartite approach based on cooperation between Government, Unions and Business, perhaps along the lines of the Dutch model – which has worked well there. Nevertheless, full scale questioning of the existing political culture and announcing a major inquiry to generate system alternatives did not happen in his period, or since. Sadly, Rudd and the six ALP Premiers also failed to use a great opportunity to replace the Federation.

The conservative PMs, Abbott and Turnbull, have not presented any innovative governance system reform. Abbott toyed with the idea of reducing the states to administrative agencies of the Federal Government (first mentioned at a conference in Tenterfield, October 2008 which I attended - and was given exactly eight minutes to present a paper advocating the abolition of Federation). As PM he was persuaded to try piecemeal tinkering once again, resulting in the failed Reform the Federation Inquiry. The Liberal Party seems solidly stuck in the traditional political culture. Unless there is a major change in policy direction it is difficult to see that this party has a major role to play in shaping the future of Australia.

Meanwhile, a major shift in the old dividing class lines is happening in much of the Western word. The old right vs left culture is being questioned everywhere. The middle class is missing out particularly with the growing inequality of incomes and wealth resulting from economic rationalist ideologies and the privatisation mania. Globally 65 million refugees are on the move. A complex Middle Eastern war is still raging and has caused great havoc in several countries. The foundations of the existing national state system, now counting over 200, are severely tested. Preaching border security seems like yesteryear's language and does not solve these major global crises. The UN, an organisation also long overdue for major reform, is not coping as a peacekeeper of this system. In Australia, frequent reference is made nowadays to the "old parties" and not just by the Greens. How can Australia generate competent political leadership to deal with the mounting refugee crisis? Both Government and Opposition have sent refugees to PNG and Nauru to act as a deterrent to "boat people" rather than opting for available humane alternatives e.g. to accept UNHCR approved political refugees temporarily settled in Indonesia. The Australian

Panel of Experts on Asylum Seekers, in 2012, completely failed to suggest this as logical alternative although it was recommended to them.

Australia's several governance system problems are all inter-connected. Tinkering in just one area won't do. There certainly is a strategic order of priorities. Strategically, first off should be electoral system reform. Much has changed since Horne's *The Lucky Country* was written. Ours has become a multicultural society, a strong positive, but just how multicultural really? The 49% who apparently now want to keep out refugees and immigrants who are Islam adherents don't fit that description all that well. Furthermore, parliaments, senior ranks of the public services, the judiciary, the police and corporate boards are still predominantly staffed by people with Anglo-Celtic names.

The Donald Horne commentary

Donald Horne was a senior lecturer, later professor in the School of Political Science, UNSW. He had been editor of the *Bulletin* for several years (also of the *Observer* and *Quadrant*), and was well informed on the history and practical aspects of Australian politics. Horne was already well known then as author of the best seller *The Lucky Country* (1964) in which he criticised the quality of Australian politicians and also of business management. Horne explained the term "lucky" further in his book *Death of the Lucky Country* (1976).

> *"Australia is a lucky country run by second rate people who share its luck. I didn't mean that it had a lot of material resources ... I had in mind the idea of Australia as a (British) derived society whose prosperity in the great age of manufacturing came from the luck of its historical origins ... In the lucky style we have never 'earned' our democracy. We simply went along with some British habits".*

In that text he also severely criticised the bizarre decisions by Sir John Kerr in November 1975, the then Governor-General. (Government by caprice – the Governor-Generalate, Ch. 5). The chapter dealt analytically with the many shortcomings of the archaic, colonial constitution, and the reliance on conventions that, in Kerr's view, entitled him to remove the strongly reformist PM Whitlam.

In 1977, following the debacle of Whitlam's sacking, Horne edited and partly wrote *Change the Rules* (together with UNSW academics Sol Encel, Elaine Thompson and others), a set of essays by several well-known commentators dealing with the Constitution, Australian democracy and the electoral system.

This advice has become even more relevant today because so little has changed since then. Horne was a progressive academic, promoting changes to "earn our democracy". His conviction was unique because right through the 1970s, 1980s and the early 1990s "progressive" mostly tended to mean, "left", later it became "left" or "Green" or both. "Conservative" was the opposite; it was synonymous with "pro-capitalist". Horne didn't fit neatly in either category. His inquiring and critical mind went increasingly beyond this simplistic ideological divide.

In 1977 a minor constitutional change was made by Malcolm Fraser's government. This was to ensure that vacancies in the senate would go to the same political party whose senator had vacated the seat. Up to that amendment political parties were not even mentioned in the Constitution a situation which had made it possible for the conservative Premiers of Queensland and NSW to fill such vacancies with anti-Whitlam candidates. By 1990, under the impact of neo-liberalism and the ending of the Cold War, the overarching left vs. right dichotomy began to wane. The threat to and protection of the environment began to take over. Constitutional and system change went into the "too hard" basket.

Remarkably, the ALP Whitlam Government, that came to power in 1972 after 23 years of conservative Governments, did act fast to introduce some significant reforms. Although most of them seemed to "frighten the conservative horses", the incoming Coalition Fraser government, after 1975, repealed none of them. Nevertheless, constitutional reforms failed to be introduced after 1977, such as the federal recognition of local government and an important Section 128 amendment. Sadly, the preceding extensive Inquiry into Constitutional Reform, from 1985 to 1988, ended with four failed amendment referendums. If this was not enough the failed minimalist Republic Referendum, in 1999, made constitutional reform practically impossible, without very strong popular pressure – which didn't exist.

Horne favoured a Republic for Australia, discussed in *The Lucky Country* and *The Next Australia*. He advocated a minimalist Republic, as did the Australian Republic Movement later, in the early 1990s, and apparently still does. However, Horne saw it "as happening within a radical national framework" (Davies, G., 2011), and approached it from a quite different mindset. The ARM's current belief that Australians would still only want an Australian as a symbolic Republican Head of State, and no other major governance reforms, is seriously questionable. Should an Australian Republic continue to be governed by nine parliaments, nine public services, a negative adversarial political culture and obvious lack of reformist leadership? The decline in support for the Republican cause, as a minimalist project, is at least in part explained by that very attitude. It would make sense for Australians to now consider a *maximalist* Republic, the essence of an Australian Political Science Association Conference Paper I presented in Canberra as long ago as 1992.

In *Change the Rules* (1977) Horne also referred to the Swedes who successfully rewrote their 1809 constitution in 1974. He said we don't need to wait until we have a major crisis; and it doesn't have to take long either. That is now 40 years ago. Here is the final para of his Chapter 1 in *Change the Rules*:

> *"We have brought out this book to stimulate public discussion not only because our Australian constitution provides an inefficient instrument for modern government, and contains no liberal provisions, and, so far as representative democracy is concerned, is professedly undemocratic. We have also brought out this book because there are within the constitution, interpreted literally, the elements of civil discord and political chaos."*

Australia is not using the competence that is available

The dangers of an essentially two-party parliamentary system, staffed by often mediocre politicians and combined with a dysfunctional, costly federal system, should be obvious. This combination ensures that an inordinate amount of time is spent, often wasted, by the major parties on finding fault with each other, "playing politics". It is the cause of frequent inability to arrive rapidly at sound decisions about major infra-structural works, new national policies, or even to arrive at sensible solutions at all. The Constitution of 1901, more broadly the "Rules" in Horne's terms, is frozen in time and colonial conventions. It does not mention the PM, and provides no guidelines at all regarding the involvement in wars. Thus, the unmentioned PM can take the country to war without any democratic backing; there is no **requirement** for a mandate, no parliamentary debate even, no plebiscite, and no referendum. Just a phone call from the US President will do! This is how Australia was drawn into the Iraqi disaster, the Afghan conflict and earlier Vietnam. Horne's 1964 book was seen as a "kick in the pants" of the Australian Government and business management. It was, but did not result in major changes then, and not after the questionable dismissal of a reformist PM in 1975 either. There is no shortage of real competence but it is too often not available for political leadership.

At least four obvious problems should be dealt with and be presented for public debate. If no political party is game to start the ball rolling could we appeal to the ABC to start the media debate? After all, the public broadcaster has education as a definite major role in its charter! BUT, since the election of Tony Abbott as PM, in 2013, the ABC has been steadily politicised with a series of deeply conservative appointments at senior levels. Nevertheless, the Managing Director has the authority to launch political information programs, surely. That should go well beyond Current Affairs. Current Affairs are happening within the existing governance systems. Political information can be about changing governance systems. That means education for the general public. The SBS actually does more in this field already and may have to continue on its own along this path if the ABC fails to live up to its own Charter in this respect.

Questions about three major areas for governance reform, not counting the Republic.

1. **The electoral system.** Why not proportional representation – open party list system, based on multi-member electorates for the House of Representatives?

2. **Federal – state relations** – a costly problem. The expense of maintaining Federation is up to $50 billion each year. Why not replace it with a two-tier system: a national and strengthened local government level, with regional clusters?

3. **Aspects of Westminster system** e.g. the practice that Ministers have to be in and of the Parliament, meaning they have been elected as MPs. Most other systems provide for appointment of functionally competent Ministers from **outside** the legislature.

Electoral reform is probably the key to all other major reforms. Why continue with a single-member-electoral district system that produces the adversarial, negative, undemocratic and unstable two-party system? In reality, Australia is governed by the dominant faction of one of the major parties, representing perhaps 30%. This ridiculous, totally undemocratic situation was again highlighted by the Same Sex Marriage issue: 61% in favour, more than twice the conservative Coalition faction.

The initial principal remedy here is to introduce Proportional Representation (Open Party List System) for the next House of Representatives election. This is used widely in the world but is not very well known in Australia, which only uses the Hare-Clark system of PR which originated in England but is not used there. New Zealand had a Royal Commission into electoral systems in 1986 and opted for Party List, first used in 1996, now already 20 years ago. This is common practice in 86 countries; it results in Coalition Governments and a quite different political culture whereby parties need to seek common ground to form majorities. Splinter groups and factions would move away from the majors and form their own parties, achieve separate representation and voice. Major parties would avoid unproductive adversarialism. If we want young people to come back to the political arena that reform would be *the* primary remedy. The Government, through the Australian Electoral Commission, surely could provide an inexpensive booklet to educate the nation and then introduce the required legislation. As long as we have states these could become *multi-party* electoral districts. Or the larger states could be sub-divided in somewhat smaller multi-member electoral districts, for starters.

The Westminster system is defined as a representative parliamentary system in which the Ministers are "in and of the parliament". Citizens cannot be Ministers unless they are elected to Parliament as MPs. This virtually ensures that most Ministers are often functional amateurs. In the UK the choice is from 600 MPs, minus the Opposition MPs. In Australia's federal Parliament it is 150 MPs, minus the Opposition MPs. This fusion between the political executive and the legislature is a real problem. The competence of Ministers, both at the federal and state levels, often leaves much to be desired. Amazingly, Ministers are even frequently moved from one portfolio to another, reshuffled. Some have several portfolios. Should it not be a prime objective of reformers to improve the quality of Governments and political leadership? Surely, therefore it would be much better for the party executives to be able to choose from the entire society. There are a huge number of outstanding potential candidates out there but they would not bother to go through the tedious party pre-selection process and then be involved in election campaigns. The Westminster system rules such people out to serve he nation as principal legislators. As major party membership is now around 0.5% of population this is a very serious situation indeed. The pool from which to select leadership potential is just very small. It is true of course that many MPs have a law degree and many others have a trade union background, mainly as union officers. Does this provide sufficient functional qualification to be an effective Minister?

Separation of powers very desirable

Why should the Government have to be "in and of the Parliament", as the Westminster System culture prescribes? Apart from the UK and some of the British Commonwealth countries Ministers are generally NOT "in and of the Parliament", a very healthy arrangement. In such countries Ministers may be called to the legislature, to explain government policy or to answer questions. Or they may sit in the Parliament, of their own volition and preference, to listen to the debates but they are not members of it and don't vote in it. These so-called "extra-parliamentary political executives" are the rule in all non-Westminster systems, both in the US and all European, collegiate parliamentary systems, obviously excluding dictatorships. The domination of the Parliament by the Government AND the front bench of the Opposition in the Westminster system detracts greatly from the principal role of the House of Representatives. In Australia this system has turned the Parliament into a complete farce at times. Just how much longer do the Australian people have to suffer this situation?

Australia's archaic 1901 constitution was certainly meant to be a flexible democratic document to be adjusted with the changing times and circumstances. Section 128 and the federal structure made that fairly difficult though but the most formidable barrier was thrown up by the evolving two-party system after 1910. The existing two-party system was solidified by the 1918 and 1924 Commonwealth electoral acts. In practice, ever since that time, proposed amendments needed both major parties to agree on them to achieve the double majorities required by section 128. Just eight out of 44 passed. Australians should understand that their single-member-district electoral system not only causes major parliamentary obstacles but also blocks constitutional change. Add to that the requirement that voting in referendums is also compulsory and the picture of ever deteriorating system stagnation becomes crystal clear.

Chapter 4

a. **The Constitutional Inquiry of 1985 – 1988 – the Referendum questions. What happened to the rest of the Report?**
b. **The problem of Section 116 – "Freedom of Religion"**
c. **New attempt at law reform has started.**

a.   The Constitutional Commission of 1985 – 1988

A serious attempt to review the Constitution was actually made by this Commission. Its members were: Sir Maurice Byers QC, Professor Enid Campbell, Hon. Sir Rupert Hamer, Hon. Justice John Toohey, Hon. E. G. Whitlam, QC and Professor Leslie Zines. The Commission was assisted by a number of expert advisory committees:

- Executive government
- Distribution of powers
- Trade and national economic management
- Individual and democratic rights under the Constitution
- The Australian judicial system

This is not the place to examine in detail what ground was covered.

It can be said that it was an extensive examination and that the need for it was not in doubt whatever. Economic management, distribution of powers and human rights were given much attention and quite detailed recommendations followed. In the end, the question of what could be put to the people in a Referendum as a first serious attempt to "update" the Constitution, with some hope of success, was a vexed question. Considerable debate occurred as to the legal capacity to change the Constitution altogether, outside Section 128, as the Constitution was still "encased" in British constitutional law and practices. The role of the (British) Australia Act (s) of 1986 gave rise to much discussion among constitutional lawyers but it was inconclusive. The following four questions were finally put to the voters:

1. ***Constitution Alteration (Parliamentary Terms) 1988*** proposed to alter the Australian constitution such that Senate terms be reduced from six to four years, and House of Representative terms be increased from three years to four years. It also proposed for the fourth time that Senate and House elections occur simultaneously.

2. ***Constitution Alteration (Fair Elections) 1988*** proposed to enshrine in the constitution a guarantee that all Commonwealth, State and Territory elections would be conducted democratically.

3. ***Constitution Alteration (Local Government) 1988*** proposed to alter the constitution so as to recognise local government.

4. ***The Constitution Alteration (Rights and Freedoms) 1988*** was proposed legislation that was put to referendum in the **Australian referendum, 1988**. The legislation sought to enshrine in the Australian constitution various civil rights, including freedom of religion, rights in relation to trials, and rights regarding the compulsory acquisition of property.

Initially, three of the proposals, put by the Hawke Government, had tentative bi-party support for these proposals, but this was withdrawn altogether during the campaign. In the end, the Coalition parties opposed all four proposals. The highest national vote was 37.6 % for the "Fair Elections" question. Once again it was demonstrated that constitutional referenda fail unless they have the full support from both major parties. The major parties basically gave up for the next 30 years!

However, following this failure a number of academics and a few political journalists started making various cases for rewriting the Constitution altogether, including the author of this book (APSA *Newsletter* 66/1993). Journalist David Solomon, as well as academics Helen Irving and George Williams attempted to move away from piecemeal tinkering. Solomon, in his 1999 book *Coming of Age,* called for the radical overhaul of the Australian Constitution in order to achieve an effective Republic. Here is a small part of an extensive review by journalist Tony Stephens.

"Solomon's proposals would bring major changes to Australia's version of the Westminster system of government, reviving the doctrine of separation of powers between parliament, government and the judiciary, and restoring power to the people. They include:

- A parliament of only one house that would have primary law-making powers

- Ministers would be selected on merit, from outside parliament, to form the government

- A bill of rights would protect peoples' rights and freedoms

Solomon comprehensively rejected the conservative guidelines 'if it ain't broke, don't fix it'. He argued that Australia's system is in "desperate need of repair and must be fixed if Australia is to prosper". The most radical of the suggested changes was that "the (directly elected) President should have powers similar to the US President". This 1999 book was published too late to have a major impact though - one month before the Referendum.

Opinion polls showed however that Australians are not keen on a US style President. After the election of President Trump this would be even less so one could assume.

Helen Irving, a constitutional historian (UTS and Sydney University) devoted the 2001 Barton Lecture to the constitutional issue.

"The (1901) Constitution was written in response to a wide range of interests and wishes. People knew and understood the debates, and when they looked at the completed product, they saw in it almost nothing that they did not recognise. This is not the case today. The Constitution is probably unintelligible to most Australians in 2001. I don't mean unintelligible because the vast majority has never seen it, let alone read it. I mean, even if they had seen it - indeed, particularly if they had seen it. .... Australia's relations with Britain have undergone many changes since 1901, and a range of sections, which refer to the old imperial ties, are no longer operative. The Empire - once a great and familiar idea to Australians - is scarcely remembered, let alone understood.... many of the institutions created and authorised by the Constitution are described in confusing and even misleading ways. What they do say depends upon a body of unwritten conventions and lies largely 'between the lines... many of the issues of the 19th century are not the issues of today'."

George Williams (2002), a well-known UNSW Law Professor, provided five reasons to rewrite the Constitution:

1. The Constitution is out of touch with political reality. He argues that the people know very little about their Constitution, that "it was not written as a people's Constitution but instead as a compact between the Australian colonies to meet the needs of trade and commerce, among other things". So, for instance, it says very little about it is to be Australian ...how we should behave towards each other as human beings and as Australians". The text of the Constitution does not match political reality because it is premised upon an understanding of the Westminster system of government operating in the United Kingdom".

2. The Constitution has failed the Australian Indigenous peoples. They played no part in the drafting of it and, when it came into force, explicitly discriminated against them, section 51 (26). They are in fact regarded as "outsiders". Reconciliation cannot be successful unless this is rectified.

3. The Constitution doesn't serve the economy well. Although High Court interpretation has enabled the federal parliament to control and regulate the national economy, the federal vision contained in the Australian Constitution is now inconsistent with modern understandings of the Australian economy. Williams writes, "our economy does not consist of discrete and insular sectors of commerce within each state or even within Australia" (the implication of Section 92 which says guarantees that trade, commerce and intercourse among the states shall be absolutely free). In reality it exists within a world of global markets ..."In order to compete effectively on a global scale, given our small population and geographical location, Australia requires national laws on issues ranging from industrial relations to consumer protection and trade practices".

4. The Constitution is almost totally deficient in the areas social justice and human rights. Williams places great emphasis on this deficiency. That is understandable because many other shortcomings can be challenged from this very perspective. The framers of the Constitution chose to rely on the operation of the Common Law but it is now quite widely accepted that this is indeed very inadequate now.

5. The text of the Constitution suggests that Australia is not an independent nation, argues Williams. This is beyond dispute. Section 2 in particular makes it clear that the Queen is the Head of State and the Governor-General is the Queen's representative. This is the very opposite of an independent Republic. The symbols provided by this Constitution are those of a Monarchy of another country of which Australia is a sub-ordinate overseas Dominion.

Several other academics and writers added significant contributions to the idea that major changes are required. Patmore, G. & Jungwirth, G. (2002) edited a series of "Labour Essays" entitled *The Big Makeover – a new*

Australian Constitution, Pluto Press, which included the Chapter by Williams. In 2004 Hudson, W. and Brown, A. J., scholars of Griffith University, edited *Restructuring Australia – Regionalism, Republicanism and Reform of the Nation-State*, Federation Press, which contains contrasting chapters by those advocating major changes as well others defending the status quo or favouring minimal change. The three books by Harris, B. (2002) *A New Constitution for Australia*, Ashgate-Gower Asia Pacific; Harris, B. (2012) *Freedom, Democracy and Accountability – A vision for a New Australian Constitution*, Vivid Publishing; Harris, B. (2014) *Exploring the Frozen Continent, What Australians Think of Constitutional Reform*, Vivid Publishing; Winterton, G. (2001) - *Republic Resurrected*, The Federation Press, and Saunders, C. (2003) (2nd ed) – *It's Your Constitution – Governing Australia Today*, The Federation Press, should also be mentioned; and Ward, A. "Trapped in a Constitution: The Australian Republic Debate" (*Australian Journal of Political Science*, Vol. 35, No. 1, pp. 117-123).

There are many other constitutional complications. Just a few are summarised here:

Apart from the overriding issues flowing from the archaic federal structure there are several other issues that require solutions:

The Corporations Power:
That power is laid down in Section 51. It restricts the Commonwealth power to legislate in respect of matters, which are specifically provided in the Constitution. E.g. the Federal Government only has a power to legislate in respect of FOREIGN corporations. This means that the power to deal with national corporations is vested in the states - obviously a serious limitation for the national government. In order to overcome/bypass this problem the National Scheme laws have been enacted in 1989/90. There are four laws that govern this system. There have been complications with this system that many corporate leaders want sorted out - principally by making the Corporate Power a federal concern altogether.

(Source: Andrew Taylor, "From Wakim to Hughes", *Law Society Journal of Western Australia*, October 2000).

Income tax:
Since WWII Collection of Income Tax (the main source of revenue for Governments) has been centralised, first as a temporary measure but subsequently it became a permanent feature. The Howard Government has

tried to put the clock back by handing the GST revenue to the states. Is this the way to go?

Tertiary education:
Financed and policy determination by the Federal Government. However, organisation, legislation, governance, etc. is a concern of State Governments. Does this make sense?

Expenditure on health:
Divided between Commonwealth and States resulting in endless squabbles and inadequacies, e.g. hospital funding.

Investment:
Most states have independent investment strategies, promotion and offices (permanent trade commissioners, Premiers making extensive and expensive tours to sell their states). They are looking for and encouraging foreign investors. The foreign investors naturally exploit this inter-state competition and end up with, usually, exceptionally good deals - at the expense of Australia as a whole. Is this what a small nation of 24 million can afford to do?

Distribution of Goods and Services Tax (GST) to states:
Has increased the dependency of the states on the Commonwealth. Often the quite unequal distribution of GST income amongst the states has caused much concern. This issue has received new attention as revenues of the Federal government are falling short of budgetary requirements.

The lack of human rights guarantees and Indigenous recognition.

This was partly overcome by the Racial Discrimination Act, 1977. Amazingly, the Abbott government initially moved to change this Act by changing Clause 18c in a way that would make the expression of bigotry legal. While this plan ran into considerable opposition, the existence of constitutionally guaranteed human rights and Indigenous recognition, dignity and equality would have made such an objective virtually impossible. The campaign has failed in fact.

In summary, the Constitution

1. Describes a status of dependency on Britain a situation that for all practical purposes ended after WWII in 1945. The formal position of the Governor-General is that of Her Majesty's powerful principal servant - essentially a colonial relationship. The position of Prime Minister is not even mentioned. Amazingly, decisions on committing

the country to a war are left to this Prime Minister. There is no requirement for parliamentary approval or even discussion, or any participation by the people in the form of a plebiscite or referendum.

2. Made provision for a federation, a structure of state, which made good sense in 1900 but is now a costly hindrance to effective government for a mere 24 million people. Local Government is not even mentioned in this Constitution. It has no formal relationship to the national government.

3. Hardly mentions the existence of political parties - the reality of the political system. As a result of the single-member-district electoral system, which exists separate from the Constitution, an inefficient two-party system has developed.

4. Has no Bill of Rights, the only Commonwealth country that has no such statutory protection of the rights of the Australian citizens.

5. Makes no provision for the reconciliation with and representation of the Indigenous Peoples. Recent moves to address this situation have come to nothing thus far.

6. Makes no provision for the protection of the environment a most important new value, which needs to be expressed and safeguarded.

7. Makes no provision for the election of a diversity of representatives to the two Houses of Parliament, nationally and in the states. It hardly reflects a multicultural society frequently said to be major strength of Australian society even by the current Prime Minister Malcolm Turnbull.

8. Makes no provision for the appointment of Cabinet Ministers from outside the legislature, as is the case in most European countries and in the United States. As a result, Governments are frequently lacking in quality and expertise.

9. Does NOT state that the Government derives its authority from the people's sovereignty - the very essence of democracy - and that of a Republic.

10. Does not elaborate on the nature of popular and national sovereignty and does not provide guidance as to how, for instance, economic sovereignty is to be safeguarded and promoted in a globalised world.

11. Is embedded in several constitutional conventions (usages), which are open to a variety of interpretations. Conventions should ALL be codified for them to be widely accepted.

12. Parliamentary democracy, often praised in Australia as a positive constitutional feature, is in fact NOT protected in the Constitution.

13. The position of women and the issues of equality between the sexes and of gender in Australian society is not addressed anywhere in the Constitution.

14. Given the continued discrimination of women in management and executive roles – and in political parties – this issue needs constitutional recognition.

15. Very few people are familiar with the Constitution. Most who study it find it a seriously flawed, archaic document and don't understand why we still have it. Most people have no sense of ownership of it.

16. It is practically impossible to amend the Constitution, due to the provisions of Section 128, the two-party system and the requirement that amendment initiatives can only be initiated by politicians!

17. Many leaders in the corporate sector of Australia are rightly very disenchanted with this Constitution. The Corporation Power in Section 51 is, in practice, used mainly in respect of foreign corporations (with a few exceptions). The states regulate corporate affairs, with sometimes major differences between them, a costly and frustrating situation.

18. *"Neither the Constitution nor the Commonwealth Electoral Act, 1918 nor the electoral Act of 1924 provide for democratic elections – a century of delusion".* This is the title of an article by Dr. Anthony Gray, S.L. in Law, USC. "the Constitution provides no express guarantee of a universal franchise," he claims.

To this list should be added the problems of Section 116, an issue that gained new prominence following the recent Same Sex Marriage campaign, postal survey and final decision by Parliament to make same sex marriages legal in Australia in December 2017, see below.

There was a further Constitutional Centenary Conference in 1991.

This was followed soon by the ALP National Conference decision in 1991 to push for an Australian Republic instead. Approval at a Republic referendum would necessitate significant constitutional change even with a minimalist proposal. However, the ultra-conservative proposal failed in 1999. The people clearly wanted a directly elected President. Conservatism prevailed again.

There comes a point that conservatism ceases to be a positive. It would seem that point was reached in 1999.

b. The problem of Section 116 – "Freedom of Religion"

Law Professor George Williams has stated his belief that religious liberty needs further protection as it is not adequately provided by Section 116 in the Federal Constitution. This issue has gained additional importance since the passing of the of Same Sex Marriage Bill. The outcome of the Postal Survey, passed by a majority of over 61% in favour, in December 2017, led to a Draft Law designed by Liberal Party MP Dean Smith, which was passed in its original form by the House of Representatives, and later by the Senate.

Wikipedia provides the following information on Section 116:

> "The product of a compromise in the pre-Federation constitutional conventions, Section 116 is based on similar provisions in the United States Constitution. However, Section 116 is more narrowly drafted than its US counterpart, and does not preclude the states of Australia from making such laws.
>
> Section 116 has been interpreted narrowly by the High Court of Australia: while the definition of "religion" adopted by the Court is broad and flexible, the scope of the protection of religions is circumscribed. The result of the Court's approach has been that no court has ever ruled a law to be in contravention of Section 116, and the provision has played only a minor role in Australian constitutional history. Among the laws that the High Court has ruled not to be in contravention of Section 116 are laws that provided government funding to religious schools, that authorised the dissolution of a branch of the Jehovah's Witnesses, and that enabled the forcible removal of Indigenous Australian children from their families Federal Governments have twice proposed the amendment of Section 116, principally to apply its provisions to laws made by the states. On each occasion - in 1944 and 1988 - the proposal failed in a referendum."

The Conservatives in Federal Parliament contemplated to attempt to include a general protection in the Same Sex marriage law or to enact a separate religious bill in the new year (2018). Nothing came of this initially mainly because PM Turnbull didn't want to spend further time on discussing detailed amendments of this nature in the dying days of 2017. Moreover, the celebratory mood that came over Parliament discouraged further haggling. However, as Williams also warns in his article, the Section 116 jurisdiction does not cover the states. Again, the federal structure provides scope for instance, for state governments to ban the burqa, close Moslem schools and generally to restrict freedom of religious expression.

Willliams writes further *"Australian law fares poorly when it comes to religious liberty. The International Covenant on Civil and Political Rights spells out the international consensus on the need for protection. This is reflected in the national laws and constitutions of every democracy, except Australia"* (*SMH*, 21ˢᵗ November, 2017).

It is hopeful however that the Parliament's Joint Standing Committee on Foreign Affairs, Defense and Trade has this year also conducted an inquiry into "the status of the human right to freedom of religion or belief". The results of these deliberations will hopefully also be discussed next year. However, we need to understand that Standing Parliamentary Committees are made up of predominantly major party politicians whose self-interest and party discipline limits their capacity sometimes to innovate.

What happened subsequently to the Report of the 1985 – 1988 Inquiry?

Nothing much really. Regrettably, this happens far too often to major Official Inquiries and Reports in Australia. This particular Report can be found in Libraries and Universities where it is available above all to understand a detailed range of shortcomings and, to some extent also, why such efforts at reforms fail. Failure to approve the four referendums is not due to the lack of intelligence and determination with which Australian experts have applied themselves. It is due to governance system failure! Also, at that time the voters were misinformed by politicians which was possible because (1) voters, at that time, sufficiently trusted them (2) the lack of knowledge of these constitutional issues amongst voters was insufficient to go against the advice of politicians.

The principal culprit in this case was the political party system, especially the adversarial nature of that system still reflecting a society divided by capitalists and workers. This clearly does not suggest an egalitarian society at all! Quite the opposite. That is why an overhaul, a complete rewrite, that needs to happen does not come to fruition! It is essential that the electoral system, reinforcing these class opposites, has to be changed first before other reforms can succeed. Australia has to introduce a new political culture into the legislatures and also much greater competence in the Ministries. As explained in the Introductory chapter the case for major constitutional change is obvious but our thoughts need to focus on how action for change can be generated.

c. New attempt at law reform has started

Fortunately, a comprehensive renewed effort at law reform, reflected in the 2017 publication in a book of essays delivered at an ANU Law Reform Conference in Canberra in April 2016, *New Directions for Law in Australia*, is most encouraging. In that book Part V deals with Public Law and the contributions by Graeme Orr and Scott Stephenson. Also of Lael Weis, Gabrielle Appleby and Anna Olijnyk. Below are two quotes from the Introductory chapter.

> "Initial chapters argue for meta-reforms: ways to reform the process of law reform itself. Graeme Orr's chapter takes on the vexed question of compulsory voting in constitutional referendums. Orr argues that, given the distinctive nature of constitutional law and reform, voting at constitutional referendums should be voluntary. Scott Stephenson's chapter also rethinks constitutional referendums. His solution to the problem of Australia's stalled process of constitutional change is the use of citizens' assemblies – randomly selected, rigorously informed and demographically representative bodies empowered to draft referendum questions".

Clearly what these academics are arguing here is to "reform the constitutional reform system", without doubt a help but there is much more to it! **In particular, what is missing here is any connection with the electoral system, the federal structure and dysfunctional Westminster practices.**

> "As dramatic as Orr and Stephenson's reforms would be, the next two meta-reforms arguably would be even more fundamental. Lael Weis compares the culture of constitutional reform in Australia to that of the United States, where a 'popular constitutional culture' sees many or even most Americans deliberate about the meanings and directions of their founding document. Weis advocates approaches to help 'cultivate' an Australian popular constitutional culture. Gabrielle Appleby and Anna Olijnyk in turn consider an important set of cases where the constitutionality of a legislative Bill is uncertain. Their proposed reforms aim to enhance parliamentary constitutional deliberations. "

Chapter 5

The interconnection between the electoral system, the federal structure, the Republic and the archaic Constitution.

A strategic approach to achieve major governance system reforms is urgently required. Dr. Bede Harris (Charles Sturt University) has recently presented intelligent reformist suggestions to that end. He also published a book in 2002 advocating a *New Constitution for Australia*. Based on useful later research, he published two further texts in 2012 and 2014. Some commentary on this approach will follow. It seeks to demonstrate that there is a certain strategic order that could facilitate the process. Assuming that a particular end purpose is indeed desirable, the logic of the phases has to make sense. However, the underlying thinking by Harris is that the achievement of a Republic, while desirable, is not of primary importance. Also, that a Republican form of state may be more easily achieved if other major governance system changes are either achieved earlier or at the same time. In other words, what Harris argues is that Australians increasingly may find that there are other major governance problems to be fixed now and that the question "What kind of Republic?" has become a much more important and urgent issue than in 1999. Electoral reform is of a high priority order as the current Single-Member-District (SMD) system often does not at all yield democratic outcomes – and is basically responsible for the two-party adversarial system in most lower houses. The resulting frequent mud-slinging was even demonstrated again by both major party leaders at the Bennelong by-election in December 2017 (in spite of the civilised behaviour of the two candidates involved). There has been very little recognition in Australia of the interconnectedness between governance systems when it comes to reforms, even at the highest political and academic levels. This is really not only the case with the average voter. Many university graduates lack this understanding, even students who have majored in political studies and/or law.

However, the intelligent research that Harris and his team did to test voters' views on governance systems, also aimed to ascertain how much respondents really understand about the governance systems that shape Australian political structures. Clearly, that knowledge is quite basic, and often barely adequate to provide meaningful answers without further follow-up questions. Lack of relevant education undoubtedly plays a role in finding informed opinions. Plebiscites and referendums are not always the best way to test public opinion either unless questions are very well prepared and discussed by the media. The Brexit debacle is a typical example of that. The titles of the two relevant Harris books are *Freedom, Democracy and Accountability – A vision for a New Australian Constitution* (2012) and *Exploring the Frozen Continent* (2014). Both these books present the constitutional and associated problems in an easy to understand fashion. As a constitutional law academic Harris has a wide experience with constitutional and governance changes and stresses in several other systems, South Africa, Zimbabwe, Ireland, New Zealand and Australia. The 2012 book has an encouraging but cautious Foreword by former High Court Justice Michael Kirby who was also Chairman of the Australian Law Reform Commission (1975 – 1984). In the same book Harris recorded a discussion with former Senator Brandis about the importance of teaching all students about the Constitution, not just law students, how it works and how it defends and advances democracy (assuming that it actually does). Brandis displayed a somewhat elitist approach while Harris favours much wider knowledge about the Constitution resulting in a sense of ownership and pride – something that is **seriously** lacking in Australia. However, Harris writes

"it would be wrong to think that lack of engagement in constitutional debate means that voters are satisfied with the way government functions in Australia. Indeed, quite the reverse is true. Public opinion polls and public commentary both reflect an increasing dissatisfaction with the political process. Both the major political blocs (Labor and Coalition) are perceived as relentlessly negative" (p. 4)

The 2014 book starts with a survey rationale which is to find out what respondents actually understand of the Constitution and governance systems and what they want from it (shown in full in Chapter 9). The Survey was conducted by the Organisation Research Unit of the Charles Sturt University. The Survey differs from others in that it sought respondents' views on a wide range of possible reforms: electoral system, a Bill of Rights, accountability of government to Parliament, federalism and an Australian Republic. There is little doubt at all that, while the understanding of many sections of the Constitution is very sketchy, the preferences for change are very obvious and mostly not catered for. A most telling question perhaps is: do you think that school students should be taught more about our Constitution? YES 95%; No 5%!! There is clearly a strong interest in proportional representation; and also in a Bill of Rights. The interest in an Australian Republic and the abolition of the federal system is recorded as fairly low in this Survey. What was certainly highly preferred was that constitutional conventions should be codified.

A critical outcome of the Survey, Harris concludes, is that the

> *"Australian public is not as averse to constitutional reform as is commonly assumed provided that sufficient background information is given to respondents to enable them to understand what they are being asked".*

There were no questions about multicultural representation in decision-making roles in this Survey. As to electoral reform Harris favours the MMP system used in New Zealand, rather than the PR Party List systems used in far more countries (86 in fact). In the Survey question about the electoral system people are able to express what they feel about their relationship to a local representative, the essence of the Anglo SMD system. This remained moderately important. The New Zealand MMP proportional system has accommodated this sentiment. Harris probably has no personal experience with the pure Party List systems used in very many countries and he probably believes that this system is too far removed from what Australians are used to to advocate its adoption here successfully. In a later lecture to the Parliament staff in Canberra he has gone back to the in Australia known Single Transferable Vote PR system (STV, also known as Hare-Clark System) used in Tasmania and ACT, presumably because Australians have experience with these systems. My own view is that Australia should move away from both STV and SMD systems completely, which in Australia also requires compulsory preferencing. Voters have demonstrated abundantly, for many years, that they don't want to engage in preferencing candidates and parties about whom they often know next to nothing. The STV system is used in very few countries, essentially all English-speaking, and is basically only effective in very small assemblies and legislatures where voters have a reasonable knowledge of the capacities and political views of the candidates. The PR Party List systems, in contrast, based on multi-member districts, require the voter to vote for one candidate of his or her choice. Local Government in such countries is exactly that, concerned with local issues; it is not a part concern of a local federal or state MP who is often a member of a party that the citizen has NOT voted for!

Significantly, Harris also referred to the work of the Civic Expert Group in 1994 to prepare a study for civics education. This resulted in a publication in 1997 for the civics and citizenship curriculum *Discovering Democracy*, while commendable in terms of describing how the Constitution worked, lacked a critical approach. For post-school civics education, the Constitution Centenary Foundation (established in 1991) produced literature for the 1999 referendum, which was informative for the purpose but also lacked a critical approach. Regrettably, the Foundation only had a 10- year life span while there was so much more work to be done once the Referendum failed.

Chapter 6

Multicultural Australia needs to be represented, democratically and fairly. Governance systems have to change to accommodate that objective to ensure social and political cohesion.

In this text emphasis has been placed on recognition of serious shortcomings of the Constitution and political systems in a rapidly changing society. This situation was first realised in 1975 and failed to be remedied ever since. Already prior to the minimalist approach to creating a Republic during the 1990s this awareness surfaced again and was expressed widely, particularly among political scientists. Further concern about that conservatism and continued dominance of Anglo-centric values and systems surfaced in several publications in the early noughties. Professor Hugh Emy, by no means a radical scholar, wrote in 1994, now 23 years ago,

> *"Demographically and culturally, Australia is moving away from its Anglo-Celtic origins. As it does so, issues of social cohesion and political integration naturally become more important: what features or symbols of 'Australianness', of Australian national identity, can best unify and motivate an increasingly heterogeneous, multicultural society? Are symbols and institutions inherited from Britain adequate? (One should bear in mind, too, that many Australian of Celtic origin oppose the latter). This aspect is related to Australia's changing geopolitical orientation. As Britain has sought its future in Europe, so Australia must develop its economic and strategic links with East Asia. One may ask, "what will best promote such links?' The perception in Asia that Australia is still, at heart, a British creation and offshoot? Or the sense that Australia is consciously trying to create a new identity in both the region and the world?"*

At the closing weeks of 2017 one could add: Is Australia continuing to play the role of a staunch ally of the US, based on a WWII inspired ANZUS Treaty, in relation to power dynamics of the emerging Asian power blocs? Given that we now have some 35 American military and intelligence units in Australia is it not time that we start thinking about a more neutral foreign policy position? Are we actually supporting the rapid and extensive US military build-up in South Korea to counter possible North Korean missile threats? Who in fact determines such Australia's Asian policy orientations today?

Australia has adopted various policies to promote multiculturalism since 1972, starting with the initiatives by the Whitlam Government that also opened up a dialogue with China. However, several government systems and cultural practices in Australia do not adequately assist in preserving and further promoting the multicultural society. This is an increasingly important issue in that, recently in various parts of the world multiculturalism has acquired a somewhat negative connotation, e.g. in several European countries. Also, the harsh policies of both our major parties in respect of political and religious refugees arriving by boat are not in harmony with the values underpinning our multicultural society. Governance systems that will be identified as being in need of reform, from this perspective, are the electoral systems, the Australian Constitution, representation in our parliaments and executive levels of corporations. Multiculturalism has generally been a remarkable success in Australia presenting a positive model to the world. The recent crisis related to asylum seekers has raised serious questions about the sincerity of and capacity for cultural tolerance. Community responses to radical Islam expressions and violence appear extreme and polarise the society. Without quite major reforms in governance systems and representation the conflicts and intolerance demonstrated could stimulate latent prejudices and endanger social cohesion in Australia. In this context, the criticism by former Senator Brandis when the One Nation Senator Pauline Hanson recently turned up in a burqa in the Australian Senate stands out as a courageous public call to responsibility required by politicians as well as others. He rejected her behaviour candidly and pointedly, thereby setting an example that was applauded particularly by the Opposition and given wide media coverage.

Multiculturalism in Australia is a remarkable national strength that deserves to be celebrated, preserved and promoted. To his credit Prime Minister Turnbull has understood that and frequently refers to it. It has contributed much to social cohesion, harmony and economic development.

But does he always practice what he preaches? What is happening in the country in recent years and, equally important internationally, threatens such values. For a country that played such an important role in the formation of the United Nations in 1945, was recently a non-permanent member of the

Security Council, and has just been elected as a member of the UN's Human Rights Commission, the promotion of racial and cultural tolerance, as well as human rights, are essential objectives. However, government systems, cultural practices and policies in Australia do not sufficiently assist in preserving and further promoting the multicultural society. Political representation of ethnic minorities, although slowly improving, has been inadequate for a long time. Highly skilled ethnic immigrants, especially of Asian origin, also have considerably difficulty in reaching executive levels in corporations. Achievements of post WWII migrants, although qualitatively perhaps somewhat different compared to those of the settled population, are only sparsely rewarded in annual honours lists.

The policy of Social Inclusion, promoted by the ALP after 2007, was supposed to assist multiculturalism but initially appeared to replace it. The earlier proposed further commercialisation of the SBS detracts from the very important role of the Special Public Broadcaster in achieving cultural diversity, broadcasting in no less than 74 languages (Pomeranz & Dempster, April 2015). Plans to merge the ABC and SBS would also seriously reduce SBS's contribution. The senseless closure of the ABC's Australia overseas network greatly reduces interaction with and exposure to Asian and Pacific countries. Attempts by the Abbott government to remove section 18c of the federal Racial Discrimination Act are indicative of an underlying desire to accommodate racial prejudice although couched in a desire for extending "freedom of expression". In NSW, the Migration Museum is still not a reality, if it is to happen at all. In recent years the concerns about political refugees arriving by boats and their treatment in detention camps in Pacific countries has raised serious questions about the multicultural values of Australian society, here and internationally. The Constitution in particular neither reflects the multicultural realities and aspirations nor protects the human rights of citizens and newcomers. The absence of a Statute of Liberty or Bill of Rights at the federal and most state levels is a further handicap. Historical celebrations such as Australia Day, the elaborate ANZAC commemoration and the Magna Carta event are representative primarily of Anglo-Celtic Australian culture and experiences. Nevertheless, Australia has in reality become a microcosm of a growing multicultural world. It is not a melting pot. The earlier policy of assimilation was wisely shelved in 1972 by PM Whitlam. That resulted in a growing appreciation of cultural diversity as well as meaningful social cohesion. What happens here can and should be an important positive example for the rest of the world. Currently, national governments sometimes seem to have lost sight of that. Asylum seekers are treated like hostile "illegal" invaders by a growing number of citizens, a threat that requires "border protection", as if Australia is at war. While there have been serious attacks by small extreme Islam groups Australia should not lose sight of, or endanger, the generally very positive record. The preparedness to accept 12.000 refugees from Syria is in keeping with that positive record. Nevertheless, as a consequence support for political parties of the extreme right have grown considerably, overseas and in Australia. Regrettably, it has dominated Government since 2013. The pressures of these trends on our major parties' policies in respect of asylum seekers arriving by boat threaten the values claimed to underpin our multicultural society.

From Social Inclusion to Political Inclusion to Social Cohesion and Political Cohesion

Multiculturalism in Australia resulted from the necessity to broaden immigration policies to include non-Anglo immigrants soon after WWII e.g. Greeks, Italians, Dutch and Germans. After the White Australia policy was abandoned altogether several other nationalities were invited as well. The philosophy of multiculturalism in Australia simply means that approved immigrants from any country can become residents and then Australian citizens and that all ethnic groups are valued for their cultural diversity and contributions to Australian society. The initial Assimilation Policy, based on the expectation that all immigrants would soon fully adapt to the existing way of life, was abandoned by the Whitlam Government in 1972 as both unrealistic and counter-productive. It was replaced by the Multiculturalism Policy and promoted enthusiastically by the then Immigration Minister Al Grassby. After the Whitlam Government lost the election in 1975, the incoming conservative Fraser Government fully maintained this progressive policy. It thus became a bi-partisan policy until the Howard Government came to power in 1996. Howard, a critic of multiculturalism adopted what he called a "One Australia" Immigration and Ethnic Affairs Policy (launched in 1988, following a trip to Margaret Thatcher's Britain). Some multicultural innovations were either scaled down or abolished altogether. Essentially, it aimed at ending multiculturalism and Howard also opposed a treaty with the Indigenous people. Apparently, the Coalition parties feared a fragmentation of the society and conflict. In reality, the multicultural policy was characterised by tolerance and engagement. Altogether Australia's increasingly diverse migrant communities have brought with them interesting food, lifestyle and cultural practices, as well as different languages that enriched the wider society immeasurably. It also greatly stimulated young people to travel to other countries where they learned to appreciate other cultures and values. This secondary effect is rarely acknowledged.

Nevertheless, during the Howard period two proposals to guide and police religious diversity saw the light of day. Furthermore, by 2007 a large number of immigrant nationalities had settled here regardless, including from Africa, the Middle East and several Asian countries. The cultural diversity was further stimulated by a growing number of Asian and Pacific students attending universities. Although paying substantial fees for their education, making tertiary education the third largest export earner, Asian students frequently had to put up with racial discrimination at major universities in Melbourne and Sydney. Meanwhile, political representation remained largely the prerogative of the settled population. Political inclusion was a concept rather foreign to the major parties. Political cohesion would remain increasingly illusionary.

The introduction of Social Inclusion as a new major ALP policy initiative after 2007 may have been, in part at least, a response to the conservatives' fears about expected multicultural fragmentation. However, it was also a response to genuine welfare needs of new ethnic groups and, promisingly, it replicated a somewhat similar initiative in Britain (by Prof Charles Leadbeater). The latter emphasized the need for full participation in society by all. Several major conferences were held up to 2012 to assess the meanings of Social Inclusion as well as the connection between Multiculturalism and Social Inclusion. I attended one such conference, in June 2009, organised by the Inner & Eastern Sydney Migrant Interagency (IESMI). The program's title was *Multiculturalism and Social Inclusion - Information and Strategy Forum on Cultural Diversity and Social Justice.*

Key speakers were Senator Ursula Stephens (Parliamentary Secretary for Social Inclusion) and Professor Jock Collins, UTS. Senior administrators in the multicultural field presented interesting papers about Ageing/Disability, Community Services, Education/Training, Health, Housing, and Settlement/ Refugees. The principal message seemed to be that Social Inclusion covers far more than the earlier multicultural agenda. Several of around 130 delegates remarked, mostly to their surprise, that multiculturalism, as a key concept seemed to have been overtaken by Social Inclusion. The discussions were certainly lively. The philosophy of "Social Inclusion" was originally approached by the ALP in a key document in 2007, as a remedy to "Social Exclusion", described as follows:

> "Labor believes that to be socially included, all Australians need to be able to play of full role in Australian life, in economic, social, psychological *and political terms*. To be socially included, all Australians must be given the opportunity to:

- secure a job

- access services

- connect with others in life through family, friends, work, personal interests and local community

- deal with personal crisis such as ill health, bereavement or the loss of a job, and

- *have their voice heard*" (emphasis added)

However, the later "Principles" document presented by the new Social Inclusion Board, again offered merely a strong social welfare orientation. There was no mention of multiculturalism or cultural diversity here. There was also no concern about the role of the employee in the workplace as an individual who may want to democratically participate in the ownership of and decision-making in the business enterprise. This has long been the practice in many European countries. Strangely, this is still not seen as an important aspect of "Social Inclusion" in Australia even though Minister Julia Gillard clearly advocated that approach:

> *"The concept of social inclusion in essence means replacing a welfarist approach to helping the underprivileged with one of investing in them and their communities to bring them into the mainstream market economy. It's a modern and fresh approach that views everyone as a potential wealth creator and invests in their human capital. Including everyone in the economic, wealth-creating life of the nation is today the best way for Labor to meet its twin goals of raising national prosperity and creating a fair and decent society. This is a recognized policy ambition of social democratic parties around the world today. Fairer workplace laws that encourage enterprise bargaining and cooperation will help create a fairer and wealthier society, but on their own they are not enough. We need a new approach to social and economic policy too. And social inclusion is it ".*
> *Gillard, J. (2008).*

More recently "Social Cohesion" has emerged as a critical concept connected to multiculturalism. The prominence of the rise of Islam in Australia may be the particular background to this development currently. Many immigrants and refugees from Islam countries arrived, following conflicts in which Australians troops were actively involved, notably in Iraq and Afghanistan. Currently adherents of Islam are estimated at 2.2% of the population. Cohesion can be more specifically defined as "the tendency for a group to be in unity while working towards a goal or to satisfy the emotional needs of its members". This definition includes important aspects of cohesiveness, "including its multi-dimensionality, dynamic nature, instrumental basis, and emotional dimension". (Carron & Brawley, 2000)

Obviously, a multicultural society as exists in Australia, is an adequately socially cohesive society where loyalty and pride in one's ethnic and/or religious group can coincide with both pride and loyalty in Australia as one's country and nationality. The exception that may have occurred here initially, with a very small minority of the Islam religion, is that they placed Sharia Law above the essentially secular Constitution of Australia. Where this became a real problem a PM (Gillard) suggested that "these individuals could exercise the right to leave the Australia". She argued that Australia is a secular country where freedom of religion exists but not at the expense of the Constitution itself. By all accounts these are exceptions. Most of the Islam clerics and the overwhelming majority of Muslim adherents actually have no such problems.

Nevertheless, a minority of Australians, even including non-Muslim immigrants of Non English-Speaking Background (NESB), have embraced extreme anti-Islam positions such as supporters of One Nation and Australia First. In my own Dutch Australian community I have found some immigrants expressing and circulating quite uninformed alarmist views. These seem to reflect prejudices emerging from European countries, including the Netherlands, where refugee numbers are much higher than in Australia. Clearly, such views do NOT advance community cohesion in Australia. I have countered such views referring also to the truly remarkable career of Ms. Ayaan Hirsi Ali, an exiled feminist from Somalia who, for some years, was even a prominent MP in the Netherlands. A widely read author she has also lectured in Australia a number of times (2007, 2008, 2010). In a recent ABC TV interview, she reminded viewers that there is no separation between Church and State in the Islam religion as is quite common in Western countries. Islam is indeed a very political religion, perhaps comparable to absolutist Catholicism in Europe until the Protestant rebellion. The Dutch Republic fought the Spanish King for 80 years over this, until 1648! And won! Such an experience does not have to be relived again. Proper Government information and education is the remedy here.

However, quite disturbingly, the most important attack on social cohesion in Australia flows from the attitudes of the current Australian Government in respect of terrorism by the "Islam State" (ISIS) and other countries. The so-called "war on terrorism", waged first by the Abbott Government against Muslim individuals who are "radicalized" by complex anti-Western movements in the Middle East could, if it persists, damage social cohesion in Australia.

The claimed intention is to make Australia a country safe from terrorism. One such measure is under serious consideration, the cancellation of Australian citizenship by holders of dual citizenships. Individuals who participate in cooperating with the "Islamic State" would lose their citizenship, on the basis of intelligence provided by Australian Security and Intelligence Organisation (ASIO) and a decision by the Immigration Minister. An amendment to the Citizens Act, it is suggested, would achieve that purpose.

Political representation and inclusion – a neglected aspect of social cohesion

It was believed by some that the 2010 Hung Parliament would yield a "paradigm shift". Did it mean the end of one party ruling and the other opposing no matter what? In most other representative democracies, a number of parties seek cooperation to form majority government providing a quite different political culture. But unless concerted action to change the electoral system was taken Australia would soon be back in the adversarial mode. This is exactly what happened after the 2013 federal election when the Coalition first led by Tony Abbott came to power. Participation in Parliaments by NESB candidates, especially in lower houses, is still very poor. Women are also under-represented especially in the Liberal Party. Only one Green sits in the House of Representatives, Indigenous people are hardly represented. Although recognised by Australian Governments as deficient, progress towards greater diversity in parliaments has been very slow. This has much to do with the Single-Member District (SMD) electoral system and compulsory preferential voting. Here is a 1989 statement from the *National Agenda for a Multicultural Australia:*

The issue, in 1989: "*The cultural diversity of Australia is not reflected in the key decision-making institutions of society. This is particularly true of our formal political structures. The representation of women, Aboriginal people and people from non-English speaking backgrounds is poor at all levels of the Australian political system. Elected representation at the municipal, State and Federal levels of government does not mirror the ethnic composition of the total population. At the State and Commonwealth levels, for example, only 7% of Parliamentarians are from non-English speaking backgrounds. Aboriginal people and women are similarly under-represented. Remedying this situation depends in part on broader issues affecting social and economic equality, as well as on proportionate participation in political party processes and on the pre-selection policies of the parties themselves*". (Jupp, J.,1989)

The issue, in 2006 - 17 years later! In a later, very comprehensive and detailed paper published by the NSW Parliamentary Research Library, the following conclusion reads:

> *"The purpose of this paper has been to highlight some of the complex historical, theoretical and structural aspects hindering the capacity of parliaments to reflect the cultural diversity of the Australian community. At present, ethnic and racial minorities remain disproportionately under-represented in legislatures around Australia. The debate surrounding the appropriate level of presence of ethnic and racial minorities in legislative chambers revolves around questions of democracy, equality and recognition. It gives rise to the threshold question of which groups deserve representation, and how are these groups to be defined? There are no simple answers and matters are complicated further by the fact that many people have multiple group identifications and that groups can come into being and then fade away. Essentially it is a question of the balance that needs to be struck between the representation of minorities, and the maintenance and development of an overarching sense of national identity and purpose."* (Anthony, K., 2006).

That conclusion is somewhat surprising because the paper shows very convincingly that ethnic, and racial minorities remained politically under-represented in Australia. The most obvious question that requires to be asked, so many years later, is WHY? Yes, it is an issue of democracy, of fairness and equality, but not really one of "balance". There may be a simple answer. The major problem is the SMD system. Anglo-Celtic candidates have better chances to be elected in winnable seats and, thus far, the major parties have not been prepared to change that. The SMD system favours mostly male traditional "Aussie" candidates, not ethnic minority candidates unless they are representing a very strong minority in an electoral district. This does happen in a few instances and the major party then takes advantage of that situation from within its own ranks (major membership less than 0.5% of the population!). Proportional representation (PR), especially the party list system, would end the SMD system problems. However, PR as proposed in this text does NOT aim at ethnic group representation. PR has multiple advantages. Still, the replacement of the SMD system by multi-member electoral districts would undoubtedly open up greater opportunities for individuals of different ethnic, cultural and religious background, also for women and Indigenous candidates. The pre-selection process would no longer be the virtual monopoly of the major parties. Diversity of representation would be served.

The Australian adversarial two-party system is altogether increasingly dysfunctional. It often cannot readily achieve parliamentary majorities where they exist and are badly needed. The obvious recent example is the carbon price issue. The refugee policy is another one. Federal-state relations a third. Currently, Australia is governed by the right-wing faction of the Conservative Coalition. That group has a small majority in the Coalition of two conservative parties jointly representing approximately 30% of the total national electorate. The so-called "small l liberals" have to tow a party line that they frequently dislike but politicians crossing the floor is extremely rare. Party discipline and loyalty prevent it. Calls for a Centrist Party are heard, especially in South Australia, but Centrist parties cannot get up in sufficient strength in Australia given the SMD electoral system. Small Centrist parties have come and gone in recent decades. The lessons should by now have been learned.

The 2009 Electoral Reform Inquiry's first Green paper explained *correctly* that **diversity has increased greatly in Australian society since 1945. This is hardly reflected in the Parliament though. But the second Green Paper actually discouraged major system reforms, in spite of exactly what is needed.** Apart from the lack of diverse representation there is another very detrimental drawback, often not realised or mentioned. The two-party dominance has thwarted many efforts to update the Constitution. Proposals for referendums, **initiated exclusively by politicians here**, need support of both major parties to be passed in terms of Section 128.

Overall 90 countries use a PR system, 86 the Party List variety. In Europe, nearly all use proportional representation (list systems), except the UK. Where new constitutions were introduced in the last few decades PR was mostly adopted and **often enshrined** in the constitutions themselves. This was the case in Portugal (1974), almost all of the countries behind the former Iron curtain in Eastern Europe (after 1991), the new South Africa (1996) and also in New Zealand. 90% of the PR systems are "Party List". **This means that the political parties present a list of candidates and the voters place ONE mark next to the party and a particular candidate (at the same time) to indicate the preference for their party AND the candidate.** Clearly, this system would serve a multicultural society and would serve Political Inclusion and Cohesion. This information is freely available on the Internet to anybody who is interested in it.

The Greens have the PR policy in their platform but have not campaigned on it much. Obviously, it would be greatly in their interest to do so. They are grossly under-represented in lower houses. Changing the Commonwealth Act of 1918 can simply introduce PR at federal level. **No constitutional amendment is required.** The introduction of PR would change the political culture of this country for the better. It is a fairer system, much more democratic, simple for the voters, easier to count, less expensive and it provides diversity, flexibility and new ideas in our parliaments. Pork-barrelling would end; bye-elections would end. Above all, it would enhance political and social cohesion and suit a multicultural society! Several Liberal Party leaders have said "Liberals need more women and ethnic candidates". Referring to the oversight of business woman Dai Le for pre-selection for the Legislative Council, Premier Mike Baird said that the "Liberal Party must be representative of the whole community" (*SMH*, 22.6.2015). It is much easier to achieve that by means of proportional representation than by quotas.

When checking the NSW and federal MPs by surname, in late June 2015, the following percentages showed up:

NSW Legislative Assembly:	Anglo-Celtic names:	80%
	Others:	20%
NSW Legislative Council:	Anglo-Celtic names:	74%
	Others:	26%
House of Representatives:	Anglo-Celtic names:	86.7%
	Others:	13.3%
Senate:	Anglo-Celtic names:	80.1%
	Others:	19.9%

Names are sometimes not indicative enough but the federal parliament also provides a list of countries of birth. Of the 226 Members and Senators the record is: 26 overseas born of whom 17 come from English-speaking countries. On that basis only nine of the 226 were themselves born in Non English-Speaking Background (NESB) countries (late 2015 figures).

Recent newspaper articles have presented the problem of multicultural under-representation at federal level in a different way. Eryk Bagshaw wrote "if Parliament was a suburb, it would be amongst the least diverse in the country" (SMH, 7/12/2017). He found that the forced citizenship declaration of MPs not only revealed those with, often remote and or unknown, dual-allegiances but has also allowed us to see for the first time if the diversity of the Parliament reflects a multicultural Australia. His conclusion: **"In short: no, it does not. It is not only overwhelmingly white and male, but chronically underrepresents a growing Asian population, while over-emphasising the proportion of Australians born with British and European heritage."** Thus, PM Turnbull's claim that Australia was the most successful society in the world" has not transferred to the seats in Parliament. Bagshaw found that 40% of politicians have at least one parent born overseas compared to

53% of Australians; 0.8% of parliamentarians are of Middle Eastern descent, compared to 1.4 % of the country; and 0% of politicians have a parent born in China or India, compared to 3% of Australians.

Again, it should be realised that this situation is largely the result of the SMD electoral system because, over the years, the major parties have tended to field Anglo-Celtic candidates in winnable seats because most seats have majority Anglo-Celtic populations. To field ethnic minority groups candidates, especially in marginal seats, is risky. This situation also is not at all attractive for immigrants originating from non-Anglo backgrounds as they have little chance of being pre-selected. Actually, often this has little to do with racial or ethnic discrimination by party managers. **It is a realistic calculation resulting from the system.** Proportional representation, based on multi-member districts – and one vote only instead of preferential voting, demonstrably results in more diverse representation. It makes for Political Inclusion and therefore for Political and, through that, Social Cohesion.

Internationally Australia is being watched with considerable anxiety and reserve. Kelly Tranter reported on this in an article in the eJournal **Independent Australia** on 14.12.2017, as follows:

> *"Australians are repeatedly told by our Government that 'We are the envy of the world when it comes to strong border protection policies'. Yet heavily redacted documents relating to our bid for the United Nations Human Rights Council, released under Freedom of Information laws, suggest that in diplomatic circles the view is that our border protection policies create a reputational vulnerability, resulting in a defensive position against the increasing pressure of the world. Consecutive immigration ministers and prime ministers confidently assert that Australia has found the solution to border protection issues and proudly spruik this glorious news to all those parts of the world struggling with similar issues. Few take them seriously."*

Regrettably, in a section of Australian society today values of multiculturalism are little more than skin deep. This would not be all that important if the political impact of that relatively small minority was not as significant as it is within the context of Australia's adversarial party and parliamentary systems. It provides sufficient support for the deeply conservative factions of the governing Coalition parties that often pursue policies that are not representative of the multicultural society. These policies also have the effect of damaging Australia's good international reputation on multiculturalism and, contrary to their, at times, misguided xenophobia, actually threaten to diminish existing social cohesion. The remedies suggested in this text are to be sought in major electoral and constitutional reforms rather than border protection, and harsh treatment of refugees in other countries to deter legitimate refugees and people smugglers. Multicultural Australia undoubtedly has the talent and will to progress opportunities and, given a chance, get the country going again.

Representation of the Indigenous people is of course an issue of a different order. Regrettably, the treatment of the Indigenous peoples has recently been given the cold shoulder again by the Prime Minister, following the Uluru conference proposals for a Treaty and an advisory role to Parliament. In a recent ABC Q & A program (December 2017) Mr. Turnbull was severely tested by the audience and could not provide a satisfactory explanation. Constitutional renewal requires full Indigenous participation.

It could well be a much more plausible solution to the political inclusion and representation of the Indigenous people to include them as full partners in the negotiations for a new Constitution.

Conclusion

This book is about action for major constitutional change. It also aims to present an assessment of the continuing inaction since 1975 and the reasons for that. It aims to show to those many in Australia who are not familiar with governance systems why this stagnation is blocking progress in many areas. Why is it so and how can it be changed for the better? What is presented here is a categorical rejection of conservatism, adversarialism, federation and the continuation of the existing governance systems. These are now both unrepresentative of a diverse multicultural society and/or no longer fit for use. Australian democracy needs to be restored, renewed, improved and, most definitely, also saved from spreading plutocracy and threats of corruption. The governance systems we need to renew are available. They have been tested widely. By far the largest number of national states are unitary states, not federations. Most of them are well decentralised. No less than 86 states use proportional representation - party list systems. What is proposed here is not some idealistic, new-fangled doctrine. The positive values of Westminster are used widely in most democratic states. The negative aspects of that system, especially the restriction to limit Ministries to elected MPs, should be abandoned as soon as possible if we want quality and competence to be restored in our Governments. All present Australian Governments, federal and state, are still embedded in political cultures and class representation of the late 1890s, of another country. We can do much better than that.

Totally alternative systems have been proposed in recent years, some of them funded by people with very good intentions. Understandably, they call for the abolition of existing parliaments staffed by "professional" politicians and the end of party politics. They seek the extensive involvement by citizen assemblies, supported by experts, so as to cut out political parties altogether. They reject the notion of "representative democracy" as almost a contradiction in terms. The changes proposed would be enormous and critics ask for convincing examples. The theory is perhaps attractive but examples don't really exist as yet although the Athenian Assembly may have been a small-scale forerunner. However, democratic representation in complex national states is something different from relatively small Greek cities. It has to be and can be genuinely representative. It has been emphasised strongly in this text that the major issues of our time seem to be particularly associated with countries that use the SMD electoral systems. Action for realistic change, as suggested in this text, can come from community organisations, the public and commercial broadcasters, in fact all media, traditional and social. The entry into Parliament of major system reformers is initially most likely to happen in the Senate, where the electoral system assists minor parties to gain representation and provide opportunity for a Centrist renewal movement to emerge that can spread and initiate change. The current popular rejection of the two-party political establishment should not allow reformers to overlook the potential for support for major change from amongst some of the major party politicians. Our politicians are all victims of the existing governance systems that compel them to act in ways that often don't make real sense. In particular, Australia needs to move away from the adversarial two-party system. That first essential change is possible even without constitutional amendment. It would be the first step on the road to recovery and end stagnation. Other changes would follow logically and probably quite quickly. In chapter five an explanation is provided why further major changes, blocked in the past, would follow in a strategic fashion. Centrist majorities would be much easier to generate agreement on sensible renewal measures after the adversity of the current party system has been overcome. YES, we can overcome.

Bibliography

List of books and other resources

Griffith, J. A. G. (1985) - *The Politics of the Judiciary*, 3rd ed. Fontana.

Hall, Rodney (1998) - Abolish the States, Pan MacMillan, Sydney.

Harris, Bede (2002) - *A New Constitution for Australia*, Ashgate-Gower Asia Pacific.

Harris, Bede (2012) - *Freedom, Democracy and Accountability – A vision for a New Australian Constitution*, Vivid Publishing.

Harris, Bede (2014) - *Exploring the Frozen Continent, What Australians Think of Constitutional Reform*, Vivid Publishing.

Hennig, Brett (2017) - *The end of politicians - Time for a Real Democracy*, Unbound.

Hirsi Ali, Ayaan (2007) - *Infidel - My life*, Free Press.

Hocking, Jenny (2008) - *Gough Whitlam –A Moment in History*, Vol 1, The Miegunyah Press.

Horne, Donald (1964) - *The Lucky Country*, Penguin.

Horne, Donald (1976) - *Death of the Lucky Country*, Penguin.

Horne, Donald (1977) - *Change the Rules, Towards a Democratic Constitution*, Penguin.

Horne, Donald (1992) - *The coming Republic*, Pan MacMillan.

Hudson, W. and Brown, A. J. (eds) (2004) - *Restructuring Australia – Regionalism, Republicanism and Reform of the Nation-State*, Federation Press.

Irving, Helen (1997) - *To Constitute a Nation - A Cultural History of Australia's Constitution*, Cambridge University Press.

Jupp, James, York, B. & Mcrobbie, A. (1989) - *The Political Participation of Ethnic Minorities in Australia*, AGPS, Canberra.

Kildea, P., Lynch, A. and Williams, G. (eds) (2012) - *Tomorrow's Federation*, The Federation Press, Sydney.

Lijphardt, Arend (2012) - *Patterns of Democracy: Government Forms & Performance in Thirty-six Countries,* Second Edition. New Haven: Yale University Press, 2012.

Levy, Ron, O'Brien, Molly, Rice, Simon, Ridge, Pauline & Thornton, Margaret (eds) (2017) - *New Directions for Law in Australia - Essays in Contemporary Law Reform,* ANU, Canberra.

Lindell, Geoffrey (ed) (2007) - *The Mason Papers Speeches by Sir Anthony Mason*, Federation Press.

Marsh, Ian (1995) – *Beyond the Two-Party System, Political Representation, Economic Competitiveness and Australian Politics,* Cambridge University Press.

Patmore, G. & Jungwirth, G. (2002) - "Labour Essays" entitled *The Big Makeover – a new Australian Constitution,* Pluto Press.

Picketty, Thomas (2014) - *Capital in the Twenty-First Century,* The Bellknap Press of Harvard University.

Robertson, Geoffrey - *Dreaming too loud- Reflections on a Race Apart,* 2013.

Report of the Royal Commission on the Electoral System in New Zealand, December 1986.

Saunders, Cheryl (2003) (2nd ed) - *It's Your Constitution - Governing Australia Today,* The Federation Press.

Saunders, Cheryl (1997) - *The Australian Constitution,* Constitutional Centenary Foundation, 2nd Edition.

Stretton, Hugh (1970) - *Ideas for Australian Cities,* Griffin Press.

Walsh, Richard (2017) - *Reboot: Democracy make-over to empower Australian voters,* Melbourne University Press., July 2017.

Whitlam, Gough (1983) - *The Truth of the Matter,* Penguin, (2nd ed).

Winterton, George (2001) - *Republic Resurrected,* The Federation Press.

Winterton, George (ed) (1994) - *We, the People,* Allen & Unwin.

Wheare, Kenneth (1963) - *Federal Government, 4th ed.,* Oxford Uni. Press.

Woldring, Klaas (2005) - *Australia - Republic of US Colony?* Lulu.

Woldring, Klaas (2006) - *How about OUR Republic?* BookPod/Amazon.

Woldring, Klaas (2012) - *Australia Reconstructed.* BookPod/Amazon.

Woldring, K., Nicholas, A., Snow, J. and Drummond, M (eds) (2014) - *Beyond Federation – Options to renew Australia's 1901 Constitution,* BookPod/ Amazon.

Articles/Conference papers/On line publications

Aitkin, Don - *'The dual citizenship scandal/imbroglio/fiasco',* On Line Opinion, 17th November 2017.

Appleby, Gabrielle - *'Appointing Australia's highest judges deserves proper scrutiny'* https://theconversation.com/appointing-australias-highest-judges-deserves-proper-scrutiny-35039, December 9, 2014.

Appleby, Gabrielle - *'Let's see the Solicitor-General's advice on Barnaby Joyce's section 44 fate',* The Australian Financial Review, 18 August 2017, available online: http://www.afr.com/business/legal/lets-see-the-solicitorgenerals-advice-on-barnaby-joyces-section-44-fate-20170816-gxxza4.

Appleby, Gabrielle - *'The High Court sticks to the letter of the law on the citizenship seven',* The Conversation, 27 October 2017 available online: https://

theconversation.com/the-high-court-sticks-to-the-letter-of-the-law-on-the-citizenship-seven-85324.

Lambert, Scott - *'Not fit for purpose - re-imagining the Australian Constitution'*, The Mandarin. https://www.themandarin.com.au/86092-not-fit-purpose-re-imagining-australian-constitution/#.Wh3So2xa-fE.email.
https://www.themandarin.com.au/87610-constitution-2-0-a-new-version-of-australias-founding-law/,
https://www.themandarin.com.au/86092-not-fit-purpose-re-imagining-australian-constitution/#.Wh3So2xa-fE.email
https://www.themandarin.com.au/86529-principles-new-australian-constitution/#.Wh3Tnurc46E.email

Ward, Alan - *"Trapped in a Constitution: The Australian Republic Debate"*, Australian Journal of Political Science, Vol. 35, No. 1, pp. 117-123.

Woldring, Klaas (1992) - *"Why the Australian people must rewrite their entire Constitution"*, Annual Conference Australian Political Science Conference, Canberra (abridged version - published in *APSA Newsletter*, No. 66, September 1993).

Newspaper and media items dealing with multiculturalism and political inclusion dealt with in Chapter 6.

Allard, T. and Whyte, S. - *The poor treatment of refugees is giving Australia a reputation as a self-interested, uncaring nation, SMH*, 20.6.2015.

Aly, Anne – Panelist on ABC Q&A Program, 29 June 2015.

Anthony, K. 30/2006 . *The Political Representation of Ethnic and Racial Minorities*, NSW Parliamentary Research paper.

Simon and Schuster Carron, A.V., Brawley, L.R. (2000) - *Cohesion: Conceptual and measurement issues*, Small Group Research, 31:1, 89-10.

Fisher, Leo D'Angelo (2011) *Bamboo Ceiling - Corporate Australia remains Anglo Celtic*, Business Review Weekly, September 15 - 20, 2011.

Gillard, Julia (2008) - *Social Inclusion And Economic Empowerment*, Speech in February, 2008.

NATSEM (2010) - *Calling Australia Home - The Characteristics and Contributions of Australian Migrants, a report written by Riyana Miranti, Nino Nepal and Justine McNamara from NATSEM for the AMP*, Income and Wealth Report, 27 November, 2010.

SBS: *Preserve its Integrity! Don't Increase Ads on SBS. Internet petition organized by* Margaret Pomeranz and Quentin Dempster, April/May 2015.

Woldring, Klaas - *Are Australian governance systems and policies in tune with a multicultural society?* Advancing Community Cohesion Conference, 2015(published conference paper).

Young, Nareen & Lo, Jieh-Yung (May 2013) - *Let's Capitalise on Australia's Cultural Diversity*, in Pro Bono Australia.

Footnote: Professor Arend Lijphardt on proportional representation

Lijphart is the leading authority on consociationalism, or the ways in which segmented societies manage to sustain democracy through power-sharing. Lijphart developed this concept in his first major work, *The Politics of Accommodation*, a study of the Dutch political system, and further developed his arguments in *Democracy in Plural Societies*.

His later work has focused on the broader contrasts between majoritarian and "consensus" democracies. While Lijphart advocated consociationalism primarily for societies deeply divided along ethnic, religious, ideological, or other cleavages, he sees consensus democracy as appropriate for any society with a consensual political culture.[1] In contrast to majoritarian democracies, consensus democracies have multiparty systems, parliamentarism with oversized (and therefore inclusive) cabinet coalitions, proportional electoral systems, corporatist (hierarchical) interest group structures, federal structures, bicameralism, rigid constitutions protected by judicial review, and independent central banks. These institutions ensure, firstly, that only a broad supermajority can control policy and, secondly, that once a coalition takes power, its ability to infringe on minority rights is limited.

In *Patterns of Democracy* (1999, 2nd ed., 2012), Lijphart classifies thirty-six democracies using these attributes. He finds consensus democracies to be "kinder, gentler" states, having lower incarceration rates, less use of the death penalty, better care for the environment, more foreign aid work, and more welfare spending – qualities he feels "should appeal to all democrats".[2] He also finds that consensus democracies have a less abrasive political culture, more functional business-like proceedings, and a results-oriented ethic. The 2012 edition included data up to 2010 and found proportional representation (PR) was vastly superior for the "quality of democracy", being statistically significantly better for 19 of 19 indicators. On the issue of "effective government" 16 out of 17 indicators pointed to PR as superior, with 9 out of 17 statistically significant. These results held up when controlling for the level of development and population size.

Lijphart has also made influential contributions to methodological debates within comparative politics, most notably through his 1971 article '*Comparative politics and the comparative method*', published in the American Political Science Review.

www.ingramcontent.com/pod-product-compliance
Lightning Source LLC
Chambersburg PA
CBHW072207090426
42740CB00012B/2427